From the Desk of the Middle School Principal

Leadership Responsive to the Needs of Young Adolescents

Kathleen M. Brown
Vincent A. Anfara Jr.

A SCARECROWEDUCATION BOOK

The Scarecrow Press, Inc.
Lanham, Maryland, and Oxford
2002

A SCARECROWEDUCATION BOOK

Published in the United States of America
by Scarecrow Press, Inc.
A Member of the Rowman & Littlefield Publishing Group
4720 Boston Way, Lanham, Maryland 20706
www.scarecroweducation.com

P.O. Box 317
Oxford
OX2 9RU, UK

British Library Cataloguing in Publication Information Available

Library of Congress Cataloging-in-Publication Data
Brown, Kathleen M. (Kathleen Marie), 1964–
  From the desk of the middle school principal : leadership responsive
to the needs of young adolescents / Kathleen M. Brown, Vincent A. Anfara
Jr.
     p. cm.
  "A ScarecrowEducation book."
  Includes bibliographical references (p.   ) and index.
  ISBN 0-8108-4390-0 (alk. paper) — ISBN 0-8108-4384-6 (pbk. : alk.
paper)
     1. Middle school principals—United States. 2. Educational
  leadership—United States. 3. School management and
  organization—United States. 4. Middle school education—United
  States. I. Anfara, Vincent A. II. Title.
  LB2831.92 .B78 2002
  373.12'012—dc21

                                                    2002004581

⊗™ The paper used in this publication meets the minimum requirements of
American National Standard for Information Sciences—Permanence of
Paper for Printed Library Materials, ANSI/NISO Z39.48-1992.
Manufactured in the United States of America.

To
Robert J. and Joan E. Brown — KMB
and
Dorothy F. Anfara and Kevin E. Smathers — VAA

Contents

Tables and Figures

Foreword

It is unsettling to think that there is no quintessential method of teaching or learning. Despite the passage of time, man remains too complex to respond to a single way of imparting his wisdom and knowledge to others. Our understanding of metacognition remains as mysterious as our knowledge of metaphysics. Worst yet, society looks to its educators to unravel the conundrum while we turn our heads to the researchers.

In their work entitled *From the Desk of the Middle School Principal: Leadership Responsive to the Needs of Young Adolescents,* Kathleen Brown and Vincent Anfara have delivered an insightful treatise about education at the middle years level from the principal's perspective. Since the 1960s, hundreds of studies have been devoted to the unique characteristics of the transescent learner. In my 33 years as a public school teacher, assistant principal, and principal at the junior high and middle school levels, I have suffered through reading an enormous number of books and papers on holistic student development, interdisciplinary team teaching, thematic planning, and the importance of effectively organizing middle schools into a flow chart of particular componentry such as advisory periods, common planning time, and varied instructional strategies to name a few. One needs only to refer to *This We Believe* (NMSA, 1982) to refresh one's memory of the most important concepts that have been considered the essential framework of successful middle schooling. *From the Desk of the Middle School Principal* spotlights the role of the principal pursuant to school reform and school improvement. Currently, we are engaged in what appears to be an indictment of the middle school, the worst charge claiming that the middle school has abandoned academic rigor and is more interested in meeting the students' physical and psychosocial needs. The authors respond with a backwards glance at the role and responsibilities of teachers and particularly principals in the reform effort. The Carnegie Council on Adolescent Development in its publication entitled *Turning Points* (1989) stresses the importance of the principal's ability to provide visionary leadership. That theme resonates throughout this book as well as most of the previous and present effective schools research.

Why the principal? Certainly he or she must operate within a broad parameter of subordinate and superordinate roles and other criteria. Superintendents, school boards, teacher contracts, varying school codes, parent and community pressures—all contribute to an endless ebb and flow of policies, practices, and procedures. At some point, we must look upon the principal to interpret and respond to these pressures. That action is the "development responsiveness" that Brown and Anfara refer to as grounded leadership, the steady hand on the tiller.

Just how should effective middle school principals administer their schools in a manner that will result in high student achievement within a developmentally appropriate environment? Primarily, we begin with principals who are committed and who possess a deep understanding of middle school practice and preadolescence. Today's effective principals must be able to lay the course for continuous school improvement through the analysis of instructional practices, promoting connectedness vis-a-vis continuity of education, and inculcating an atmosphere of curriculum reform and innovation. In essence, the principal assumes the role of preceptor rather than manager. Among the major studies that have emerged through recent qualitative research, *From the Desk of the Middle School Principal: Leadership Responsive to the Needs of Young Adolescents,* is one of the few that denotes the importance of developmentally responsive leadership as translated through the role of the (middle school) principal. The National Association of Elementary School Principals, in its publication entitled *Principals for 21st Century Schools* (1990, p. 12), states that "leadership provided by the principal is essential for the development and maintenance of a school organization and climate that is consistently conducive to quality education."

In closing, remember that this book is predicated on active research by authors who have transcended from the role of practitioner and who are now serving as researchers. Further, their data are compiled from middle school principals who represent a wide range of cultural and demographic diversity. The data are specific to responses by almost 100 middle school principals and 44 interviews. The analysis will greatly contribute to the existing body of knowledge and is complemented through the efforts of the authors; the implications for teacher and principal certification programs are profound. The educational community is indebted to Kathleen Brown and Vincent Anfara for their clean and precise study. The vision of developmentally responsive leadership has just gotten clearer.

John A. Bravo, Principal
Arcola Intermediate School
Methacton School District
Norristown, Pa.

The Middle School Movement and the Middle School Principal

Although this book is primarily for preservice and practicing middle school principals, elementary and secondary principals, central office personnel, school board members, teachers, and parents will find most of the best practices discussed to be both relevant and useful. Indeed, beyond their own walls, middle schools are having a profound effect on the entire range of American schooling, K–12. The middle school's emphasis on the characteristics and interests of young adolescents, the importance of a close-knit school community, the accommodation of diversity, the teaming of teachers, and integration of curriculum have found their way into many elementary and secondary schools as well.

Specifically, this book focuses on the importance of school leadership grounded firmly in the belief that schools should be responsive to the developmental needs of their students. The distinct nature of the middle school, the appropriate responses that are required from middle school principals, and a model of developmentally responsive leadership are explored. This emphasis on school leadership is not atypical because most educational research dealing with school improvement arrives at the conclusion that excellence in education cannot be attained without effective school leadership.

The importance of such a book is heightened because of recent events, including:

- Indictments that have been levied against a less than rigorous curriculum, resulting in poor student achievement at the middle level;
- The realization and admission that most middle schools have become so in "name only";

- The recognition that one of the missing elements in middle school reform is the adequate preparation of both middle level teachers and administrators.

With this as background, the reader will find in this introduction a brief history of the middle school movement, a review of the research on the middle level principalship, and a discussion of what "developmentally appropriate" means in relation to the middle school movement. Also discussed are common terms, which can be easily misunderstood; and the research design upon which this book is based.

A BRIEF HISTORY OF THE MIDDLE SCHOOL MOVEMENT

The middle school movement has been declared "one of the largest and most comprehensive efforts at educational reorganization in the history of American public schooling" (George & Oldaker, 1985, p. 1). In 1989 the Carnegie Council on Adolescent Development noted "young adolescents face significant turning points" (p. 8). Although *Turning Points* seemed to set the stage for continuing discussion and debate on the nature and character of middle level education, the call for middle level reform was not new. Earlier reports called for change in the way school was organized. For example, the Committee on College Entrance Requirements, commissioned by the National Education Association (NEA, 1899), wrote that "the most necessary and far-reaching reforms in secondary education must begin in the seventh and eighth grades in our schools" (p. 659). This commission noted that the seventh grade was a "natural turning point in the pupil's life, as the age of adolescence demands new methods and [a] wiser direction" (p. 659).

While much of the debate focused on whether or not to keep eight years of elementary school and four years of secondary schooling (Gruhn & Douglass, 1956), high dropout rates were blamed on the difficult transition from elementary to high school. The first response to the problematic 84 organization of schools was the creation of the junior high. Appearing in the first decade of the 20th century, junior highs were hailed for their ability to prevent dropouts and to prepare students for the job market. The hope was that the curriculum, as well as the students, would be invigorated by the new organizational arrangement.

Concurrent with these developments, early psychologists like G. Stanley Hall (1905) called upon educators to address the developmental needs of their students. Hall's studies influenced Americans to accept the fact that the field of education should be grounded in psychology and that adolescence should be the subject of scientific study. The development of this new science of individual differences provided another justification for the development of the junior high. In 1918, the Commission on the Reorganization of Secondary Education recommended the new organization in its annual report:

> We, therefore, recommend a reorganization of the school system whereby the first six years shall be devoted to elementary education designed to meet the needs of pupils approximately 6 to 12 years of age, and the second six years to secondary education designed to meet the needs of pupils approximately 12 to 18 years of age. The six years devoted to secondary education may well be divided into two periods that may be designated as the junior and senior high periods. (pp. 12–13)

What is important to remember from this junior high period is the recognition that schools were to understand and respond to the particular nature of the adolescent while attempting to continue the influence of the home (Koos, 1927). According to George and Alexander (1993), "the junior high emerged, originally, as an attempt to satisfy the call for a richer curriculum than the elementary school was able to offer, and a more personal atmosphere than the high school was able to develop" (p. 285).

By the early 1960s much of the literature on the junior high noted that such schools had turned into "miniature high schools" (Johnson, Dupuis, Musial, & Hall, 1994). Junior highs had become "pale imitations of senior high schools" (Grooms, 1967). Aided by additional sociological and psychological research during the 1950s and 1960s (Bossing, 1954; Gruhn & Douglass, 1956; Lounsbury, 1960), educators judged the junior high school organization as inappropriate for young adolescents who are psychologically, socially, emotionally, intellectually, and physically at a very different place than adolescents.

Eventually, in the early 1960s the call to reform the junior high had evolved into a call for the creation of the middle school. This call was furthered with the publication in 1965 of W. M. Alexander's "The Junior High: A Changing View" in *Readings in Curriculum,* edited by Hass and Wiles; D. H. Eichhorn's *The Middle School* (1966); and W. M. Alexander's *The Emergent Middle School* (1969).

In 1965, NEA defined middle school as: "The school which stands academically between elementary and high school, is housed separately (ideally in a building especially designed for this purpose), and offers at least three years of schooling beginning with either grade five or six" (p. 5). Later the National Middle School Association (NMSA) would define the middle schools as "mainly 6–8 schools, but also 5–8, 5–7, and 7–8; based on developmental needs (social and academic) of young adolescents, organized by interdisciplinary teams, with flexible organizational structures, using varied learning and teaching approaches" (1995, p. 1).

Solidifying the Middle School Concept: The Need for a Clear Rationale

In 1969 the Association for Supervision and Curriculum Development (ASCD) established the Council on the Emerging Adolescent Learner. In 1974, after much work by both formal and informal working groups, the Executive Council of ASCD appointed a group and charged them with "developing a paper for the Association identifying the rationale and significance of the American middle school and stressing the kinds of programs appropriate for emerging adolescent learners" (1975, p. v). In 1975, ASCD published *The Middle School We Need* that reasserted the need to develop schools around the needs and characteristics of young adolescents. Recommendations such as team teaching, individualized instruction, and flexible scheduling were suggested.

In 1973, NMSA was created. In 1982 (revised in 1992 and 1995) *This We Believe* was published. This position paper sets forth ten essential elements or characteristics of the middle school:

1.   Educators knowledgeable about and committed to young adolescents,
2.   A balanced curriculum based on the needs of young adolescents,
3.   A range of organizational arrangements (flexible structures),
4.   Varied instructional strategies,

5. A full exploratory program,
6. Comprehensive counseling and advising,
7. Continuous progress for students,
8. Evaluation procedures compatible with the nature of young adolescents,
9. Cooperative planning,
10. A positive school climate. (NMSA, 1995, p. 11)

In 1985 the National Association of Secondary School Principals (NASSP) released *An Agenda for Excellence at the Middle Level*. Focused on 12 areas (i.e., core values, culture and climate, student development, curriculum, learning and instruction, school organization, technology, teachers, transition, principals, connections, client centeredness), this document aimed at building school programs responsive to the needs of students. In order for middle schools to achieve academic productivity, middle schools should be organized:

*   So that decisions are made at the lowest possible level in the organization . . . by teams of teachers working closely together with students and other school personnel.
*   So that the effects of size are minimized, large schools should be broken into smaller units or families. Schools should be organized around teaching teams that plan and work with clearly identified groups of students, thereby ensuring that every student is well known by a group of teachers.
*   With a class schedule that allows the greatest amount of uninterrupted learning time for teams of teachers working with groups of students. Teachers should be given maximum control over how instructional time is allocated and used.
*   With advisory groups of teachers and parents participating in important decisions about building goals, budget priorities, and school climate. (excerpted from NASSP, 1985, pp. 10–11)

In 1989, the Carnegie Council on Adolescent Development issued *Turning Points: Preparing American Youth for the 21st Century*. This document noted that:

A volatile mismatch exists between the organization and curriculum of middle grade schools and the intellectual and emotional needs of young adolescents. Caught on a vortex of changing demands, the engagement of many youth in learning diminished; and their rates of alienation, substance abuse, absenteeism, and dropping out of school began to rise. (pp. 8–9)

In short, *Turning Points* challenged middle schools to be places where close, trusting relationships with adults and peers create a climate for personal growth and intellectual development. To accomplish this, middle schools were to:

1.   Create small learning communities for learning,
2.   Teach a core academic curriculum,
3.   Empower teachers and administrators,
4.   Staff middle schools with teachers who are expert at teaching young adolescents,
5.   Improve academic performance of students,
6.   Reengage families in the educational process,
7.   Connect schools with communities. (excerpted from Carnegie Council on Adolescent Development, 1989, p. 9)

According to *Turning Points,* these seven components would work collectively to ensure the success of all students. Unfortunately, many middle level practitioners and researchers did not understand the ecological nature of this reform initiative. Many schools began changing the structure of their programs, adding activities such as interdisciplinary teams and advisories. Few schools adopted the reform as a total package. Although it seems common sense to assume that schools would respond to the needs of their students and create developmentally appropriate learning environments, it is evident from the history of middle level reform that schools are slow to change. But Carnegie did offer grants to 27 states that submitted competitive plans for middle school improvement. These grants helped to turn the recommendations of *Turning Points* into reality—bridging the gap between theory and practice.

Finally, in 2000 the Carnegie Corporation of New York issued a report, *Turning Points 2000: Educating Adolescents for the 21st Century.* Ten years after the release of the original *Turning Points* (1989), this report asserted as core values the following beliefs: the primary purpose of middle grades education is to promote young adolescents' intellectual development; adolescents' intellectual, ethical, and social development requires strong, supportive relationships; and successful middle grades schools are equitable with high outcomes for every student. Jackson and Davis, authors of the report, noted that the most important changes from the original report included: ensuring the success of every student, placing a greater emphasis on teaching and learning, grounding a curriculum in academic standards, and inspiring families and communities that are inextricably linked to the work of schools. While the original *Turning Points* provided a framework for middle grades educational reform, *Turning Points 2000* provided valuable guidance to practitioners interested in implementing the model.

What should be obvious from this discussion is that a very consistent collection of ideas about what constitutes a good middle school emerged. The number of middle schools increased. According to the *Digest of Education Statistics* (Department of Education Statistics, 1995), there were 9,573 middle level schools by 1993–1994. This amounts to approximately three middle schools for every junior high in existence. The most recent figures (Bradley & Manzo, 2000) document the existence of 16,000 middle schools and only 2,000 junior highs. But all too often the change was in name only, and many middle schools continue to operate as "transitional schools" (Manning, 1993).

The Reform Pendulum Swings Again

Middle schools are on the defensive. Recent articles dealing with middle level education have been replete with accounts of what is happening, especially in reference to curriculum and student achievement. The Southern Regional Education Board in March 1998 concluded that middle schools are a "weak link" in the K–12 education chain (cited in Bradley, 1998). *Education Week* published two articles attacking middle schools; one was titled "A Crack in the Middle" (Killion & Hirsh, March 1998) and the other was "Muddle in the Middle" (Bradley, April 1998). Tucker and Codding (cited in Bradley, 1998) referred to middle schools as "the wasteland of our primary and secondary educational landscape." In short, the middle school model has come under attack for supplanting academic rigor with a focus on students' social, emotional, and physical needs.

Most of the recent attacks cite evidence from studies like the Third International Mathematics and Science Study (TIMSS) and the National Assessment of Educational Progress (NAEP). TIMSS is the largest international comparative study of educational achievement to date—with approximately 500,000 students from 41 countries. Students from three distinct target populations are assessed: (1) 9-year-olds (typically grades three or four), (2) 13-year-olds (in grades seven and eight), and (3) students enrolled in the final year of secondary schooling. Focusing on the 13-year-old population, the international comparison suggests a general improvement in U.S. science scores from a 1991 assessment that placed American middle school students below average. But middle school performance in mathematics remains below the international average. In mathematics, 20 countries outperformed the United States, 13 performed similarly, and seven scored below the United States. In science, 9 countries outperformed the United States, 16 performed similarly, and 15 scored below.

Among the findings drawn from the TIMSS are the following:

- Eighth-grade mathematics classes in the United States are not as advanced and not as focused as those in Japan and Germany,
- Topics taught in U.S. eighth-grade mathematics classrooms are at a seventh-grade level by international standards,
- The content of U.S. mathematics classes requires less high-level thought than classes in Germany and Japan,
- U.S. mathematics teachers' typical goal is to teach students how to do something, while Japanese teachers' goal is to help their students understand mathematical concepts. (excerpted from *A Sourcebook of 8th-Grade Findings: TIMSS*, Mid-Atlantic Eisenhower Consortium for Mathematics and Science Education, 1997)

Reviewing the TIMSS results, Silver (1998) found "a pervasive and intolerable mediocrity in mathematics teaching and learning in the middle grades" (p. 1). Likewise, Whitmire (1998) wrote "U.S. students stagnate in seventh and eighth grades, leaving them unprepared and unmotivated for the stiff high school . . . classes looming ahead" (p. A-1).

Whereas TIMSS was designed primarily to make international comparisons, NAEP was designed specifically to measure longitudinal achievement and related demographic trends in U.S. education. NAEP data reveal that U.S. students have improved in math and reading achievement from the 1970s to the present, though science achievement remains at a level similar to that found in the early 1970s. Achievement trends for 13-year-olds differ by performance quartile. Most of the achievement gains in reading have occurred within the upper quartile, though some of the gains are in the middle two quartiles. The performance gap between White and Black students in math, reading, and science, after narrowing in the 1980s, has widened slightly across the 1990s.

Additional evidence that alarms middle school advocates comes from a variety of sources. In 1998 Johnston and Williamson investigated four communities to identify the concerns and issues of parents regarding middle schools. The analysis of 1,900 surveys, 400 interviews, and 350 exit interviews revealed that parents were concerned with:

- The pervasive anonymity in middle schools,
- The format and content of the curriculum,
- The lack of rigor and challenge of the curriculum,
- Poor instructional techniques.

Some evidence points to the lack of focused preparation for middle level teachers and administrators. Bradley (1998) wrote, "A majority of middle-grades teachers, meanwhile, were prepared either to teach elementary or high school. Most were licensed to teach elementary school, leaving them unprepared to handle more complex academic content" (p. 40).

Whatever the reasons for this current indictment, the fact remains that the reform pendulum is positioned to swing again. School districts like Cincinnati have phased out middle schools in favor of K–8 schools. How far will we allow the pendulum to swing in the movement between student-centered and subject-centered approaches to schooling? Will developmentally appropriate middle schools survive the current attacks?

A REVIEW OF RESEARCH ON THE MIDDLE LEVEL PRINCIPAL

There is a lack of research focused on the middle level principalship. Between 1981 and 1983 NASSP conducted a national study of the middle level principalship that resulted in two publications: *The Middle Level Principalship, Volume I, A Survey of Middle Level Principals and Programs* and *The Middle Level Principalship, Volume II, The Effective Middle Level Principal.* Analyzing the data from these two studies, Bauck (1987) attempted to determine the differences and similarities between typical and effective middle level principals. He concluded that although effective middle level principals are teacher-oriented and encourage parent and community involvement in the school, they do not think that formal education or participation in professional organizations have contributed to their success.

In 1999, Valentine, Maher, Quinne, and Irvin noted that the role of the middle level principal has shifted noticeably in the 20th century. More importantly they wrote, "As the principalship moves into a new millennium, characterizing the principalship with a few key words is more difficult than ever" (p. 56). Kilcrease (1995) concluded that middle school administrators perform three broad functions that enabled them to be successful: (1) providing a program especially adapted to diverse student needs, (2) promoting continuity of education, and (3) introducing needed innovations in curriculum and instruction. Additionally, middle level administrators must have the necessary skills to ensure that teaming and shared decision-making processes work well in the school (George & Grebing, 1992). Not surprisingly, several researchers assert that middle level principals should be knowledgeable about young adolescents, their development, and their learning styles (Eichhorn, 1966; George, 1990; Schmidt, 1988).

The literature about the personal nature of middle level principals is not usually research based; however, it sets forth such expectations as personal confidence (Rubinstein, 1990), trustworthiness (Tarter, 1995), and inspirational leadership (Williamson, 1991). Neufeld (1997) asserted that middle level principals, especially those in urban schools, can reform schools if they transform themselves from managers to leaders in the process of learning new knowledge and skills. Montgomery (1995) concurred that principals working with teachers can make great changes. Extending this idea of collaboration with teachers, Hipp (1997) suggested that principals could reinforce a teacher's sense of efficacy by modeling behavior, promoting teacher empowerment and decision making, managing student behavior, creating a positive climate for success, and inspiring caring and respectful relationships. Summarizing much of the research, Kellough and Kellough (1999, p. 17) provide a list of the key characteristics of effective middle school principals (*See* table I.1).

Table I.1 Key Characteristics of the Effective Middle School Principal

- Admonishes behaviors rather than personalities
- Advocates a school of problem solvers rather than of blamers and faultfinders
- Ensures a base of community support for the school, students, and faculty
- Emphasizes the importance of making everyone feel like a winner
- Encourages risk taking
- Ensures that school policies are collaboratively created and clearly communicated
- Ensures that staff and students receive proper and timely recognition for their achievements
- Ensures that teachers' administrative duties and classroom interruptions are limited to only those that are critically important to student learning and the effective functioning of the school
- Establishes a climate in which teachers and students share responsibility for determining the appropriate use of time and facilities
- Follows up promptly on recommendations, concerns, and complaints
- Fosters professional growth and development of teachers and self
- Has a vision of what an exemplary middle school is and strives to bring that vision to life
- Involves teachers, parents, and students in decision making and goal setting
- Is an advocate for teachers and students
- Spends time each day with students

THE MEANING OF DEVELOPMENTALLY APPROPRIATE

The Center for Early Adolescence's Middle Grades Assessment Program (Dorman, 1981) identified seven categories of needs that should be addressed in the organization and programs of schools responsive to the developmental needs of young adolescents. Likewise, the Carnegie Council on Adolescent Development (1989) in *Turning Points* identified eight recommendations for middle school reform, and NMSA in *This We Believe* noted there were six characteristics of developmentally responsive middle level schools. Lastly, Jackson and Davis (2000) in *Turning Points 2000* delineated seven recommendations that should characterize developmentally responsive middle schools. The recommendations of these four influential reports are compared in table I.2.

Table I.2 A Comparison of Recommendations for Developmentally Responsive Schools

Center for Early Adolescence's Middle Grades Assessment Program (1981)	Carnegie Council on Adolescent Development (1989), Turning Points	National Middle School Association (1995), This We Believe	Jackson and Davis (2000), Turning Points 2000
1. Competence and achievement	1. Ensure success for all students 2. Teach a core academic program	1. High expectations for all	1. Curriculum and assessment to improve learning 2. Designing instruction to improve learning
2. Self-exploration and definition		2. A positive school climate	
3. Social interaction with peers and adults	3. Create small communities for learning	3. An adult advocate for every student	3. Organizing relationships for learning
4. Physical activity	4. Improve academic performance through fostering health and fitness		4. A safe and healthy school environment
5. Meaningful participation in school and community	5. Connect schools with communities 6. Reengage families in the education of young adolescents	4. Family and community partnerships	5. Involving parents and communities
6. Routine, limits, and structure			
7. Diversity			
	7. Empower teachers and administrators		6. Democratic governance to improve student learning
	8. Staff middle grade schools with teachers who are experts at teaching young adolescents	5. Educators committed to young adolescents	7. Expert teachers for the middle grades: Pre-service preparation and professional development
		6. A shared vision	

The recommendations summarized in table I.2 help to answer questions related to young adolescent developmental needs such as, "What does it mean to be a developmentally responsive middle school?" What is conspicuously missing is reference to those who are responsible for the administration of these schools—the middle school principal. While there is discussion of empowering teachers and administrators, the middle level principal must play a more central role in the transformation of the school. Principals responsive to the needs of young adolescents promote and develop challenging and integrative curricula, home-based advisory programs, exploratory programs, and transition programs; and encourage teaming of teachers who use varied instructional approaches. Additionally, they encourage student assessment and evaluation that promote learning; use flexible organizational structures; and promote programs that foster health, wellness, and safety (NMSA, *This We Believe*, 1995, p. 11). But they must possess the necessary knowledge and skills necessary to ensure that these things happen. Emphasizing the importance of the principal in the process of establishing a developmentally responsive middle school, one school principal who participated in this study commented, "It is the responsibility of the principal, as leader of the school, to initiate the steps that are essential for establishing the structures needed for an exemplary middle school, like advisory programs. The principal must know what to do and how to ensure the continued success of the program."

Most discussions (NMSA, 1995, pp. 35–40; California State Department of Education, 1987, pp. 144–148) divide the characteristics and needs of young adolescents into five areas: (1) intellectual, (2) physical, (3) emotional or psychological, (4) social, and (5) moral or ethical. It should be recognized that these areas are inexorably entwined, not separate and distinct as presented. More importantly, we must remember that for the educational experiences of young adolescents to be effective they must match the nature of the group, be in concert with how they learn best, and assist them in dealing with the challenges of growing up. For example, a middle school program must recognize the great diversity of maturation that characterizes this age level and provide for differentiated instruction and cooperative learning activities.

To acquaint the reader with this connection, some of the characteristics of young adolescents and their corresponding developmentally appropriate school practices are presented in table I.3. Until recently, the emphasis has been on teachers ensuring that the curriculum is developmentally appropriate. But more importantly, principals need to ensure that their schools foster and promote practices that are developmentally responsive. Without the support and understanding of school administrators, teachers will flounder in their efforts. An understanding of the needs of young adolescents changes what school looks like and affects long established school and district-wide imposed structures, including everything from instructional practices and scheduling of classes to teacher evaluation.

There is a noticeable lack of research on the middle level principalship that focuses specifically on this issue of creating a developmentally responsive school. Several theorists (Eichhorn, 1966; George, 1990; Schmidt, 1988) assert that middle level principals should be knowledgeable about young adolescents, their development, and learning styles. But there is little written explaining how to effectively implement these developmentally appropriate practices. As noted earlier, middle school principals do not typically obtain the knowledge and skills in university-based preparation programs and have little useful professional development to fill this void. Therefore, attention must be given to the role that principals must play and the knowledge and skills they need to create schools that are developmentally responsive to the needs of young adolescents.

DESIGN OF THIS STUDY

The purpose of this book is to look closely at the world of middle level principals who are working hard at creating developmentally responsive schools. However, there may be some readers who are interested in a detailed account of how the data on which this book is based were collected and analyzed. What follows is a description of the research context and descriptions of data collection and data analysis procedures.

Research Context

Keefe, Clark, Nickerson, and Valentine (1983) described the typical effective principal as "a man . . . between the ages of 45 and 54 who

Table I.3 Young Adolescent Needs and Corresponding Developmentally Appropriate School Practices

Characteristics of Young Adolescents	Corresponding Practices
INTELLECTUAL 1. Be intensely curious 2. Consider academic goals as a secondary priority after personal and social concerns 3. Exhibit a strong willingness to learn what is considered to be useful	• Encourage the use of a wide variety of approaches and materials for instruction • Ensure a curriculum that is exciting and meaningful, encourages physical movement, and incorporates exploratories that are based in real world contexts
PHYSICAL 1. Be concerned about physical appearance 2. Experience accelerated physical development 3. Mature at varying rates of speed	• Plan opportunities for interaction among students of different ages, but with an avoidance of situations where physical development can be compared • A health and science curriculum that emphasizes self-understanding about physical development
PSYCHOLOGICAL 1. Be easily offended 2. Lack self-esteem 3. Be searching for an adult identity	• Avoid the pressuring of students by adults to explain their emotions • Activities designed to allow students to play out their emotions
SOCIAL 1. Be confused and frightened by school settings that are new, large, and impersonal 2. Be rebellious toward parents but strongly dependent on parental values 3. Display conflicting loyalties to parents and peer groups	• Arrange and coordinate the curriculum so that students may engage in service learning (e.g., community projects, peer tutoring) • Flexible teaching patterns so students can interact with a variety of adults
MORAL AND ETHICAL 1. Ask broad, unanswerable questions about the meaning of life 2. Be idealistic 3. Face hard moral and ethical questions for which they are unprepared to cope	• Provide opportunities for students to accept responsibilities in setting standards for behavior, dress, and so forth • Encourage mature value systems by providing opportunities for students to examine options of behavior and to study the consequences of various actions

Adapted from *Caught in the Middle: Educational Reform for Young Adolescents in California Public Schools.* Sacramento, CA: California State Department of Education, pp. 144–148.

has spent 10 to 14 years as a principal, 9 to 11 of which have been in his current school. The effective principals appear to be older and more experienced than the norm for middle level principals. They spend more time in professional growth activities . . . and are active in professional associations" (p. 11). The typical middle level principal in this study is a White male (78 percent), 48 years of age who holds a master's degree (73 percent) obtained in the 1970s and 1980s (80 percent). He is a seasoned educator with 13 years of teaching experience and prior administrative experience as an assistant principal (70 percent). He is certified on the secondary level (59 percent).

Sixty-six percent of the principals who participated in this study are members of NASSP, with only 36 percent belonging to NMSA. Sixty-six percent are committed to administering a middle school for no longer than five years. When assessing the responses of the participants in this study it is important to note that Pennsylvania, New Jersey, and North Carolina do not recognize middle school certification for school administrators. According to the laws in each state, a principal who is licensed at either the elementary or secondary levels may administer a middle school. A more complete portrait of the sample used in this study is available in table I.4.

The typical middle school in this study was public (100 percent), included grades six through eight (65 percent), and was located in a suburban setting (70 percent). As noted in table I.5, principals reported widespread use of teaming, interdisciplinary teaching, transition programs, exploratory curriculum, and block or flexible scheduling.

Data Collection

Data were collected using surveys and semistructured interviews. Initially surveys were sent to 175 middle level principals in the states of Pennsylvania, New Jersey, and North Carolina. Ninety-eight surveys (56 percent) were returned useable for data analysis. The surveys gathered information related to the principals': educational, professional, and personal background; knowledge of the middle school concept; experience with school reform and change; attitudes toward parent involvement in school; and knowledge of special education issues.

Table I.4 Portrait of Participating Middle Level Principals[1]

RACE/ETHNICITY	• White 76 (78 percent) • Black 9 (9 percent) • Hispanic 1 (1 percent) • Not Reported 12 (12 percent)
GENDER	• Male 76 (78 percent) • Female 22 (22 percent)
AGE	Range=28–65 years Mean=48 years
HIGHEST DEGREE	• M.A./M.S. 31 (39 percent) • M.Ed. 27 (34 percent) • Ed.D. 18 (23 percent) • Ph.D. 3 (3 percent) • BS.Ed. 1 (1 percent)
YEAR OF DEGREE	<u>1960s</u> <u>1970s</u> 3 (3 percent) 36 (37 percent) <u>1980s</u> <u>1990s</u> 42 (43 percent) 17 (17 percent)
CERTIFICATION	<u>Secondary</u> <u>K–12</u> <u>Elementary</u> 60 percent 14 percent 26 percent
TEACHING EXPERIENCE	Range=2.5–25 years Mean=13 years
PRIOR ADMINISTRATIVE EXPERIENCE	• Assistant Principal 68 (70 percent) • Administrative Experience 13 (13 percent) • Curriculum Specialist 8 (8 percent) • No Prior Administrative Experience 9 (9 percent)
ADMINISTRATIVE EXPERIENCE IN YEARS	Range=1–31 years Mean=9 years Mode=1 year (11 respondents)
TENURE FOR MIDDLE SCHOOL APPOINTMENT	• 1–3 years: 21 (21 percent) • 4–5 years: 45 (45 percent) • 6–10 years: 20 (20 percent) • 10+ years: 15 (14 percent)
FORMAL MIDDLE SCHOOL TRAINING	<u>No</u> <u>Yes</u> 58 (59 percent) 40 (41 percent)
MEMBERSHIP IN PROFESSIONAL ORGANIZATIONS	• NASSP 65 (66 percent) • ASCD 55 (56 percent) • NMSA 35 (36 percent) • STATE MSA[2] 20 (20 percent) • PDK[3] 18 (18 percent)

1. n = 98.
2. MSA = Middle School Association (state level).
3. PDK = Phi Delta Kappan.

Table I.5 Middle School Demographics[1]

SCHOOL LOCATION	Suburban 68 (70%)	Urban 19 (19%)		Rural 11 (11%)
GRADE CONFIGURATION	6–8 63 (65%)	5–8 15 (15%)	7–8 9 (9%)	7–9 11 (11%)
TYPE OF SCHOOL	Public 98 (100%)	Private 0 (0%)		Other 0 (0%)
MIDDLE SCHOOL PROGRAMS IMPLEMENTED	• Teaming 86 (88 percent) • Interdisciplinary Teaching 81 (83 percent) • Transition Programs 74 (76 percent) • Exploratory Curriculum 72 (73 percent) • Block and Flexible Scheduling 58 (59 percent) • Advisory 38 (39 percent)			

1. n = 98.

The survey contained both open- and closed-ended questions. Responses, which were scaled, were then analyzed using descriptive statistics. Unscaled (open-ended) responses were clustered into themes or categories. The descriptive statistics, used throughout the analysis, help confirm the findings.

From the pool of survey respondents, 44 principals indicated that they were willing to be interviewed. Nineteen of these 44 principals work in schools recognized as "blue ribbon" schools by the U.S. Department of Education. It is important to note that the 44 interviewees are highly representative of the larger sample of survey respondents with regard to gender, age, experience, race or ethnicity, prior school experience, and the like. These in-depth, semistructured interviews allowed the middle level principals to expand upon their survey responses, discuss more freely what it means to be a middle level principal, and explain their understanding of effectiveness in relation to middle level leadership. The researchers attempted to follow the dictates of phenomenological interviews, "to let them [middle level principals] tell us what we need to know rather than to ask them what we think, a priori, we would like to know" (Pollio, 1991, p. 4). The interviews were tape-recorded and transcribed for purposes of analysis.

Data Analysis

The process of data analysis began with repeated readings of the transcripts and the compilation of survey results. Each researcher read and reread the data to identify "the repetitive refrains, the persistent themes" (Lightfoot, 1983, p. 15), to code the data according to these emerging themes, and to make sense of the whole in terms of the context. The researchers involved in this project met to discuss and debate their individual interpretations of the data. Themes were compared and tested against the data collected. Wasser and Bresler (1996) noted that processes such as those we followed involve "multiple viewpoints . . . held in dynamic tension" (p. 6) and referred to this process as the "interpretive zone." After much discussion the seven themes that are presented in this book emerged, meeting the test of honoring the middle level principals' experiences. (By "themes" we are referring to the topics addressed in chapters 1 through 7.)

Readers will notice a number ranging from 01–44 used to identify the source of each verbatim interview account. Appendix A contains demographic information on each of these 44 principals' gender, age, race, years of administrative experience, the geographic location of their school, the grades contained in the school, and the number of teachers on the faculty.

Integrity of Data and Analysis

To help ensure the internal validity or dependability (Lincoln & Guba, 1985) of our results, we used triangulation of interview and survey data, the presentation of verbatim quotes, the use of multiple researchers (and coders), audit trails (Merriam, 1988), and member checks. The themes presented in this book were "member checked" by 12 of the 44 principals interviewed.

DEFINITIONS

Researchers note how difficult it is to conduct research in middle schools. They cite the existence of competing definitions and understandings of critical middle school components, such as advisory programs, exploratories, and teaming, as major obstacles to the research process. Middle level principals, for example, will report that their schools have advisory programs, but in many instances these are nothing more than homeroom periods. In an effort to clarify some of this confusion, the following definitions are offered.

Advisory: Advisory programs are designed to deal directly with the affective needs of young adolescents. Activities may range from informal interactions to the use of systematically developed units focused on the problems, needs, interests, and concerns of young adolescents such as "getting along with peers," "living in the school," or "developing self-concept." Advisory programs that are well designed and implemented provide young adolescents with the opportunity to know one adult really well, find a point of security in the school, and learn about what it means to be a healthy human being (Beane & Lipka, 1987, p. 40).

Developmentally Responsive Middle Schools: Developmentally responsive middle level schools are characterized by: educators committed to young adolescents, a shared vision, high expectations for all, an adult advocate for every student, family and community partnerships, and a positive school climate. Developmentally responsive schools provide: curriculum that is challenging, integrative, and exploratory; varied teaching and learning approaches; assessments and evaluation that promote learning; flexible organization structures; programs and policies that foster health, wellness, and safety; and comprehensive guidance and support services (excerpted from NMSA, 1995).

Early Adolescence: This developmental period includes individuals between the ages of 10 and 15 who experience unprecedented change, growth, and development. Changes occur socially, emotionally, physically, intellectually, ethically or morally, and psychologically. This developmental period marks the end of an individual's childhood years and the beginning of youth or young adulthood.

Exploratory Programs: Exploratories provide stimulating and enriching experiences that help young adolescents become "aware of their strengths and weaknesses and their interests before they . . .

are required to make decisions about the direction their educational careers will take in high school and beyond" (Compton & Hawn, 1993, p. 13). They were also intended to help students learn values, explore feelings, confront one's individuality, and develop respect for diversity. They are typically short in duration; provide for the active involvement of the students; and hold students accountable for completing activities, but not for mastery.

Flexible Scheduling: Flexible scheduling is designed to meet the individual needs of the student. It provides more time for in-depth investigation into topics and for delivery of a curriculum that is characterized as "challenging, integrative, and exploratory" (NMSA, 1995, p. 20). Many different types of flexible schedules have been designed: the 4X4 Block, the A/B Block, and the Fan Block are three examples (see DiBiase & Queen, 1999 for descriptions of each of these types).

Interdisciplinary Teaming: The interdisciplinary team is commonly defined as a small group of teachers from two or more academic disciplines who share the responsibility for planning, teaching, and evaluating a common group of students (George & Alexander, 1993). Researchers have found that interdisciplinary teams provide conditions that have the power to enhance teachers' beliefs in their effectiveness (Epstein & Mac Iver, 1989). Others have documented the importance of common planning time for interdisciplinary teams (Alexander & McEwin, 1989; Lipsitz, 1984).

Middle School: The middle school was conceived in part as a bridge from elementary to secondary education. It was intended to more effectively balance the subject-centeredness of the secondary school and the child-centered focus of the elementary school. Educators generally agree that grades six through eight should be included in the middle school, but there are those who believe that grade five should also be included. The proper place for grade nine continues to be debated.

Middle School Concept: The middle school concept refers to schools that incorporate curricula and instructional practices specifically designed to meet the needs of young adolescents.

These practices include: interdisciplinary teaming, advisory programs, varied instructional practices, exploratory programs, and
transition programs.

This We Believe: Published originally in 1982 and revised in 1992
and 1995, this document outlines the official policy position of
NMSA. It is considered to be a guide to "assist in achieving developmentally responsive educational programs for young adolescents" (NMSA, p. 3).

Transescents: "Transescents" is the term used by Donald Eichhorn
(1966) to represent the stage of development that begins prior to
the onset of puberty and extends through young adolescence. In
short, this is an individual in transition from childhood to adolescence.

Turning Points: Published in 1989 by the Carnegie Council on Adolescent Development, this report contains the oft-used quote: "a
volatile mismatch exists between the organization and curriculum
of middle grade schools and the intellectual and emotional needs
of young adolescents" (p. 8). *Turning Points* called upon middle
school practitioners to create small communities for learning,
teach a core academic curriculum, empower teachers and administrators, staff middle schools with teachers who are expert at
teaching young adolescents, improve the academic performance
of students, reengage families in the educational process, and connect schools with communities. All of these measures would result
in ensuring the success of all students.

Turning Points 2000: Released in 2000 and sponsored by the
Carnegie Corporation of New York, this report looks at middle
level education a decade after the original release of *Turning
Points* (1989). While the original *Turning Points* provided a valuable framework for middle grades educational reform, *Turning
Points 2000* provides more guidance to practitioners interested in
implementing the model. Readers will notice a greater emphasis
on the success of all students, teaching and learning, a curriculum
grounded in academic standards, and linkages to families and
communities.

ORGANIZATION OF THE BOOK

The heart of this book—chapters 1 through 7—describes the strategies and related practices employed by middle level principals who are struggling with implementing the middle school concept in their schools. These seven chapters are divided into three sections: responsiveness to students (chapters 1–3), responsiveness to faculty and staff (chapters 4–5), and responsiveness to school and community (chapters 6–7). This organizational structure forms the framework for our model of developmentally responsive leadership that is presented in the conclusion

In chapter 1 we discuss the principals' role in embracing the transitional period that characterizes the lives of young adolescents. In their quest for independence, students at this age struggle between parent-control and self-control. Middle level principals understand this and are both willing and able to assist faculty, parents, and students deal with issues of responsibility and accountability.

Chapter 2 focuses on parents as partners in the educational process. While research documents the numerous theoretical benefits gleaned from parent involvement, this chapter anecdotally describes the lived experiences. Seen as ambassadors, coordinators, advocates, and coop-erators, parents of middle school students can be involved in many ways. Middle level principals are not threatened by the presence of parents, but rather welcome their contributions.

Chapter 3 relays the thoughts and reflections of middle school principals as they struggle with the *Turning Points* recommendation, ensuring the success of all students. Candid comments about inclusion, special education, differentiated instruction, and the Individuals with Disabilities Education Act (I.D.E.A.) are included. Middle level principals live and instill a "can-do" attitude; they hold high expectations and find ways to make things work. They enjoy problem solving and do not hesitate to adjust, adapt, and accommodate where necessary. Their mode of response is grounded in what is best for their students.

In chapter 4 the middle level principal is presented as a partner in the collaborative attempt to improve schools for students. Middle level principals recognize the need for the bureaucratic walls of administrative construction to crumble and give way to supportive, collaborative environments that enhance professional commitment and expertise. Middle level principals listen attentively, they communicate appreciation and support, they collaborate and share decision making, and above all, they enjoy what they are doing.

Chapter 5 characterizes middle level principals as emotionally invested in their schools. They tour their school building, contribute to meetings, and attend school functions. This chapter highlights the need for middle level principals to encourage visits to other schools and classrooms, to observe great teachers, and to support long-term internships.

Chapter 6 discusses the strategies that middle school principals use before implementing reform initiatives. The process respects honesty and diversity of thought and opinion. It involves an initial exploration of possible change, followed by discussions and education regarding the issues involved. The roles of support, commitment, and ownership in educational reform are discussed in this chapter. In short, the middle school principal must share a vision for improvement and growth, work diligently at laying a foundation for change, investigate fully the rationale underpinning reform, and dialogue passionately about it.

Chapter 7 recalls the attributes mentioned in the previous six chapters and discusses flexibility as the umbrella trait for effective middle level principals. The "nature of the beast," the ever-changing, undulating temperament of young adolescents, requires a tolerance for chaos and ambiguity. Middle level principals interviewed as part of this study admitted to having an innate openness to noise, diversity, challenge, and change. They touted flexibility as the key in scheduling, role defining, involving the community, relating, and problem solving.

The conclusion brings the reader back to issues related to school leadership, and models of leadership are briefly discussed. Against this background, a model of developmentally responsive leadership is presented. Implications for the preparation of future middle school principals are also discussed.

Lastly, a list of suggested references is included in appendix B for further reading. For the reader's convenience, this list is topically organized.

Responsiveness to Students

Predicting the Unpredictable Journey to Independence: Adolescents' Undulating Nature

"Client Centeredness: The most successful schools are those that understand the unique needs of their clients and fill those needs quickly and effectively. Most important, effective schools understand the relationship of development to learning" (Arth, 1985, p. 20). The same can be said of developmentally responsive middle school principals. Chapter 1 recommends that middle level leaders embrace the challenge of this transitional period in young adolescents' lives and "ride the horse in the direction it faces" (09). In their quest for independence, students at this age struggle between parent-control and self-control. Effective leaders understand this and are both willing and able to help faculty, parents, and students alike deal with issues of responsibility and accountability. In so doing, these principals act as mediators and balance keepers between firmness, fairness, exploration, energy, developmental needs, personal relationships, and all the social aspects relevant to young adolescents. Actively recruiting student-centered teachers who are knowledgeable and committed to young adolescents is an important aspect of this task.

A POSITIVE OUTLOOK AND HIGH JOB SATISFACTION

No doubt, some principals land in administration, and in the middle school, only to discover that it is not the profession or the place for them. *Turning Points* (Carnegie Council on Adolescent Development, 1989) holds that educators "must understand and want to teach young adolescents and find the middle grade school a rewarding place to work" (p. 60). *This We Believe* (NMSA, 1995) confirms this notion of choice when it states: "Effective middle level educators make a conscious choice to work with young adolescents" (p. 13). Developmentally responsive middle level principals express a positive outlook and a high degree of job satisfaction (Clark & Clark, 1994). They are enthusiastic and optimistic!

Awareness and Satisfaction

"Schools need to meet the developmental needs of the students they serve and young adolescents are unique individuals with unique needs" (Brough, 1995, p. 33). Responsive middle level leaders are aware of this and actually view the developmental characteristics of their students as a primary attraction and source of satisfaction. They express enjoyment in working with young adolescents as well as a positive attitude toward meeting what many characterized as the "challenge" of serving as the principal of a middle school. For example, one experienced suburban principal said, "It's exciting to see them [students] enter adolescence and change from children to adults. . . . Change is something big in the life of middle school youngsters. They're going through this change, and we have to know that and appreciate that" (14). Other developmentally responsive leaders expressed similar sentiments of awareness, satisfaction, and genuine joy in collaborating with middle school colleagues to provide a positive difference in the lives of young adolescents:

Ah, it was a dream. It was something I really wanted. Middle school is where it's at for the administrator. I love being in this environment with this age group; there's enthusiasm. (24)

When the opportunity to go to a middle school was presented to me, I took it and I'm glad that I did. I love it, and I plan to stay. (28)

You need a different kind of parameter for the middle school so that you make sure it turns out right for them. It's a great opportunity to present them with successes. I just think there is just a lot of energy and a lot of willingness and readiness to learn. (09)

You need to take into account the psychological factors of early adolescents as opposed to later adolescents. We want to help the children enter adolescence with a positive self-view, good self-esteem . . . seeing themselves as successful in school and with their peers. (06)

Understanding and Responsiveness

Developmentally responsive principals realize that the middle school "is an educational response to the needs and characteristics of youngsters during early adolescence and, as such, deals with the full range of intellectual and developmental needs" (NMSA, 1992, p. 14). They agree with Manning (1993) that middle schools should be organized in such a way that they "serve the unique physical, psychosocial and cognitive needs of young adolescents by providing developmentally appropriate curricular, instructional and environmental experiences" (p. 35). They are also acutely aware that succeeding with young adolescents involves being responsive to their developmental needs—needs that are interrelated with one aspect affecting another.

Even when they discussed adolescents as a "tough age group" (27), responses were softened with statements about the principals' excitement about the challenge and/or empathy for students' developmental issues. For example, one principal advised: "You need to fully appreciate what the kids are going through and just help them. You know, be empathetic, not judgmental; don't take things personally. Remember that you're there to help them grow (13). Others agree that understanding young adolescents is vital:

I try to be patient and understanding and recognize the changes they will be going through. There's a lot of posturing going on. (16)

You have to understand middle school kids: a lot of what they do is not directed toward you, and it's not in defiance of you. It's part of their developmental scheme. (01)

In our urban school, we do a lot of proactive work through our curriculum . . . plus we have a lot of intervention work through the team. We deal with mental health issues, drug and alcohol issues. . . . So you have to take the lay of the land and figure out "are we meeting the needs of the kids?" and sort of mold your kids in a certain direction. (04)

In short, developmentally responsive middle level principals share a high degree of personal optimism. They possess a positive attitude and enjoy a great deal of job satisfaction and enthusiasm. One individual actually espoused optimism as a personal leadership philosophy. "You've got to surround kids with optimism. It's the only way. Any person learns best when they are surrounded with optimism" (07). By far, the majority of these principals work to generate optimism in others through celebrations and other forms of appreciation, realizing that creating the right atmosphere or environment is perhaps one of the most important characteristics of a developmentally responsive middle school. Interestingly, even when these principals talked about missing components of middle level education (i.e., advisories, transition programs, interdisciplinary teaching) or less-than-ideal district support, they characterized what could be considered negatives as opportunities for improvement rather than obstacles to success.

EMBRACING THE CHALLENGE

During the transition to middle school, youngsters are simultaneously experiencing many changes. According to Epstein and Mac Iver (1990), they enter puberty, change schools, revise peer and friendship groups, begin new interactions with their parents, and begin to expand their social boundaries and participation in their communities. Transitions are both difficult and exciting as they mark points of risk and opportunity for student development. One principal, in a study conducted by Bradley (1998), stated realistically: "We have the shortest amount of time with kids and the toughest time in kid's lives. It's a tough job, and it's one of the age groups that people are least likely to want to work with" (p. 41). Theme one recommends that developmentally responsive middle level leaders not only recognize but also embrace the challenge of this "undulating, transitional period" in their students' lives and "ride the horse in the direction it faces" (09). Many of the interviewees consciously chose middle school because they "enjoy this age group the most" and feel that they "make a good connection" (01). They "like their students' uniqueness and character" (12). They "are exhilarated by the challenge of their psychological and sociological development"

(13), and they are "excited about the whole middle school philosophy and working with an age group of kids that I am very comfortable with" (14).

Turning Points (Carnegie Council on Adolescent Development, 1989) and *Turning Points 2000* (Jackson & Davis, 2000) both call for middle level educators who are experts at teaching young adolescents; and for adults who are fully aware of their students' emergent characteristics and demonstrate a sound understanding of what instructional practices, activities, and strategies are most effective in working with this age group. Developmentally responsive leaders recommend "being proactive versus reactive" (35) and staying "focused on the importance of meeting the needs of this developmental age group" (34). To do so, they need a tremendous amount of energy and confidence to accept this challenge, to learn what makes the kids tick, to be empathetic, and to respond to their students' needs. A sense of humor, listening ear, open heart, versatile thought process, and a true grasp of the fundamental changes are needed.

> For me personally, I think that the kids are most challenging at this age . . . they're very impulsive, self-centered, and can be cruel to each other and to adults at times; and I think it's a neat age to work with. I try to get them to understand what they're doing, how they're doing it, and look at themselves and see if they can do it a better way. (03)

> Well, developmentally, it's where the kids are. The changes that young adolescent children are experiencing make it both extremely challenging and very gratifying to work with children of this age. I think there is a level of enthusiasm and idealism that you won't find in any other grade level. So, although they can be exasperating, they can also be a lot of fun if you win them over. (22)

> Probably because of the kids' attitudes and their zest, they're still hungry for learning in many ways and haven't become apathetic . . . the middle school youngster is developing emotionally, socially, and physically; and there are just so many things coming together that need the certain competence of a teacher, administrator, and counselor; and that makes the situation very challenging and delightful. (23)

MEDIATORS AND BALANCE KEEPERS

In-Between Dependence and Independence

Milgram (1992) reminds those working with middle schoolers that young adolescents "do a good job of hiding their fragility as they make the transition from childhood to adolescence" (p. 23). Among the needs characteristic of this formative stage are the needs to be safe, loved, accepted, recognized, and independent. It is precisely the uniqueness of these 'in-between' years that led many educators to favor the creation of a middle school. "Effective middle level educators play a significant role in helping learners understand developmental changes, the nature of changing friendships and peer relations, and shifting allegiance from family to peers" (Manning, 1993, p. 12).

In their quest for independence, students at this age struggle between parent-control and self-control. It is during this critical stage of adolescent development that middle schoolers negotiate their way toward healthy living. "They're neither adults nor children. They're trying lots of things and they're uncertain about who they are or what they're all about" (08). "I think it's a neat age to work with, most challenging ... they're now in-between" (03). Responsive leaders understand this and are both willing and able to help faculty, parents, and students alike deal with issues of responsibility and accountability. Principals work hard to create safe school environments—ones that allow children to emerge independent while supporting them in the process. They provide young adolescents opportunities for increased independence and self-direction while simultaneously setting clear limits. Heeding the advice from Bowers (1995) that the "production of the young adolescent self does not occur in isolation, and perceptive educators will recognize opportunities to play an important role in the process" (p. 102), developmentally responsive principals understand their students' need for self-exploration and self-direction and design opportunities for each of their students to establish a positive self-concept and sense of identity.

In their quest of learning to "explore, figure things out, and be risk-takers, they [middle schoolers] become accountable for their actions and make good decisions based on what we taught them and what we expect of them" (16). "When a kid is ready to accept it [responsibility], you'll know and they'll know. You won't have to dictate it to them, and you'll find that they take it naturally" (07). Principals describe a responsive environment as one that "provides young adolescents with a nourishing, open setting that allows them a little space to grow . . . space to let them be who they can be" (14). Listen to their advice to teachers, students, and families concerning this notion of being in-be-tweendependence and independence:

> I think it's the nature of the youngster. Basically, they're at an in-between age and they're not always ready to accept the responsibility for their actions. But in the struggle to become young adults and be treated as young adults, they try to divorce themselves from their parents and cut the apron strings. Yet, at the same time, they enjoy the protection and security; and they still like parent praise, although they might not admit it in front of their peers. (16)

> I think they are different from elementary students insofar as they are starting to explore issues dealing with independence. Cognitively, they're beginning to think abstractly. Socially, peer group replaces family as the major influence in their lives, and all these elements come together during the time they're in adolescence and create some pretty interesting kids. (22)

> The age is entirely different from the elementary or the high school and it's not just that they are halfway there. The maturing process that the kids go through is really quite different in the growing up that they do in middle school versus high school. Hormones kick in; all kinds of things happen to them emotionally that they don't understand. Some of their baggage is just beginning to sink in for them, so they are reflecting on that a little more . . . they are learning to be independent and well they should. They are cutting those apron strings a bit. (32)

Balance Keepers

The linkage of a school's general effectiveness to its success in addressing social and personal needs has been well-documented (Davidson, 1989; Slavin & Madden, 1989). Beane (1990), writing about effective middle schools, emphasizes that educators most successful in teaching young adolescents are those who "provide a more balanced response to the physical, cognitive, and affective aspects of learning and development" (p. 109). This balance usually requires "sustained attention" (p. 109) to the emotional needs of middle schoolers. Kohut's (1990) research on quality middle schools supports the view expressed by Beane. That is, adults in excellent schools feel a concern for the total development of students, "the total life of the student" (p. 108) and act to create an environment that nurtures this development. For, "as young adolescents strive for autonomy, as they grapple with learning how to regulate their own behavior and make responsible choices, their need for close, caring adult supervision and guidance is paramount" (Mac Iver, 1990, p. 458).

"Middle schools are for children to explore what they are interested in. It's critically important to expose these children to a variety of activities and opportunities and experiences" (08). In so doing, developmentally responsive middle level principals act as mediators and balance keepers between firmness, fairness, exploration, energy, developmental needs, personal relationships, and all the social aspects relevant to young adolescents. They understand the psychology of the young adolescent while simultaneously insisting that their young students engage in the learning process. "I'm tough when I need to be and easy when I need to be" (21). This consistency, tempered with understanding, addresses young adolescents' need for structure, "for love and security, for acceptance regardless of changes, and for optimistic perspectives on life" (Manning, 1993, p. 12).

This We Believe (NMSA, 1995) holds that "young adolescents form their sense of self in large part from the interactions they have with significant peers and adults" (p. 7). A principal's willingness and ability to enter into relationship with, to connect with, students is crucial to the developmental process. Respectful encounters, coupled with support and encouragement, validate students' emerging stories. A responsive leader is "somebody who has a lot of patience . . . somebody who can laugh at themselves and with their students . . . somebody who can see things and understand the balance between fair and firm . . . somebody who can really know when to set and hold limits" (02). Succinctly put, "Somebody who knows what to hear and what not to hear" (07).

Developmentally responsive middle level leaders are always looking for that balance, balance between the affective and the cognitive, balance between "knowing who to be tough with and knowing who to give more fuzzies to" (06), balance between the academics and the social. Responsive principals are aware that "the most important thing to a middle school kid is socialization" (07) and they make sure that they integrate that into everything they do—curricular, extra-curricular, co-curricular.

> There is a great amount of transition . . . its kind of a clash between the structure (content and curriculum) of the school and the needs of the kids, which really creates a lot of conflict. You have this clash of an academic need for a secondary setting but a need, a social need, of the kids in an elementary setting. So in that way, it's kind of exasperating and exhausting because it creates a lot of dilemmas. But yet, that's kind of a challenge and I've always been comfortable working in that area. We are unique . . . we still have to be very kid-oriented. (05)

> It's absolutely necessary that we look at the overall growth of students and well-being of the student, as opposed to just what the student learns. We need to address the middle school philosophy and deal with conflict resolution, self-esteem, study habits, career planning, and awareness . . . all sorts of issues, not just the regular curriculum. (04)

> Yes, you have to be a little bit crazy to work with them, know when to chastise and when to put your arm around them, when to stroke and when to put the hammer down. You have to understand that the kids' behavior is not directed at anyone in particular and that's just a stage they are going through. (20)

RECRUITING STUDENT-CENTERED TEACHERS

According to Duke and Canady (1991), principals need "a conception of 'good teaching' as a guide in the recruitment, selection, and evaluation of teachers" (p. 117). In their quest to hire "educators committed to young adolescents" (NMSA, 1995, p. 11), principals are reminded by Manning (1993) that middle level educators "need to plan instruction that considers the relationship between affective and cognitive learning" (p. 61). The primary expectation of any principal is that teachers facilitate learning and that students achieve understanding. In part, for this to occur, principals need to be "out there, getting involved, letting kids know them, being approachable, getting into classrooms" (30). This is true for teachers as well. As one respondent reminds us, it is important for young adolescents to know that "you enjoy them, that you're in their corner, and that you're putting them first. They sense that and they respond in kind" (22). Almost every principal in this study was oriented toward hiring student-centered teachers who are interested in both the young adolescents and the content areas they teach; teachers who are able to manage the social and emotional needs of their young adolescent learners along with their educational and intellectual needs.

Among the essential elements of a middle school, *This We Believe* (NMSA, 1995) includes educators knowledgeable and committed to young adolescents and a curriculum based on the needs of young adolescents as 2 of the 10 fundamentals of middle schools. The academic program representing the core of common knowledge recommended by the Carnegie Council on Adolescent Development (1989) suggests an integration of such subjects as English, foreign languages, history, literature and grammar, mathematics, science, and social studies. Scales (1992) argues for an equally important body of knowledge: "There is a core of knowledge about young adolescents that all who work with this age group must possess . . . middle school teachers said that knowledge about young adolescents' social relationships and self-awareness issues was especially crucial to being an effective middle grade teacher" (p. 96). The principals surveyed and interviewed for this study agree. When asked to list university courses important for middle school teachers, the respondents' top three responses were teaching methods for the middle school (54 percent), psychology of the middle level student (49 percent), and developmentally appropriate curriculum (42 percent).

Developmentally responsive leaders feel strongly that a sound grounding in psychology and pedagogy is necessary in order for teachers to feel effective in working with middle school students. Whether based on research findings or on their tacit knowledge, responsive principals clearly indicated a need for middle level teachers to first understand the students they teach and then to understand how to best approach curriculum in the middle level classroom. "You have to work with these kids differently. According to the research, they're the most difficult to work with. They have great needs and you need a certain kind of teacher to understand that, one who will address both their cognitive and their affective needs" (31). Familiarity with teacher-based advisory programs, interdisciplinary team organization, heterogeneous grouping, looping, exploratories, and flexible block scheduling, not to mention curriculum and subject content areas, is vital for principals and teachers alike.

Best Practices

The NASSP Middle Level Council, which published *An Agenda for Excellence* (1985), advocates for more student development, curriculum for middle level students, appropriate learning and instruction, client centeredness, and specifically trained teachers. NMSA, which published *This We Believe* (1995), advocates for curriculum that is challenging, integrative and exploratory along with teaching and learning approaches, assessments, and evaluations that promote learning. In their own words, developmentally responsive principals note many of these same tenets. For example, one principal responded that he "appreciates teachers who provide the best practices, allow kids to get up, to think, to use higher order thinking skills, to get away from rote memory activities, to get their hands dirty, and to create an environment where youngsters can really flourish" (13). Others agree that "students are the reason why we are here and decisions are made in the best interest of the children. We try to give students a better sense of themselves and provide them with a successful instructional program that will give them the confidence to continue to learn and remain positive" (34).

Providing a rigorous curriculum, challenging students to accomplish certain academic tasks, and clearly defining high expectations are among the best practices that enhance learning and promote achievement. *Turning Points* (Carnegie Council on Adolescent Development, 1989) advises that every student should "learn to think critically through mastery of an appropriate body of knowledge" (p. 42) and that teachers should "promote a spirit of inquiry and stimulate students to think about and communicate ideas" (p. 43). Student-centered teachers realize this and the fact that they are "working with kids that don't know what they're capable of and that the purpose of middle level programs is to allow them to explore and expand" (36). Daily they encourage their students to do and be and reach beyond to their fullest potential. Such efforts require a wide variety of strategies and a degree of comfort with different teaching methods and problem-solving techniques:

> I try to make sure that the teachers here have a fundamental understanding of the middle school child—of their characteristics emotionally and cognitively. I want them to know how Gardner's multiple intelligences, learning styles, different instructional approaches, cooperative learning, direct instruction, and project-based learning all mesh together. (21)

> You [the principal] have to be attuned to the needs of the students and the teachers because the teachers need to know how to address the middle school students. Teachers need to have knowledge of content, high vitality, be reflective, and reach beyond. They need to have high expectations for the kids and a willingness to reach beyond by constantly learning more so that they can better affect learning in the classroom. They need to be open to change. (17)

> We look at responses in their essays for their belief in a seamless curriculum for the kids, and the integration of subject matter, obviously that thematic approach. We are heterogeneously grouped; they have to address all the learners' needs in this setting. I am looking for people that have a work ethic for kids. I guess very child-centered is important. That's why we're here. (11)

Developmentally responsive middle level leaders encourage their teachers to engage in knowing themselves, their subject, and their students. It is apparent from this study and one conducted by Mills (1997) that middle level teaching "requires incredible resources of time, energy, and materials. It requires a personal commitment to teach in a variety of ways to meet the myriad needs of the young adolescents in middle level classrooms" (p. 38). This implies that, in addition to principals, middle level teachers should *enjoy* and *value* middle level teaching and young adolescents as well as their subject matter. In helping students become more independent learners and thoughtful contributors to society, the Carnegie Council on Adolescent Development (1989) contends teachers must view themselves as facilitators through which young people construct knowledge themselves. Responsive leaders are interested in what teachers do to produce inspired pupils; excited pupils; creative pupils; and pupils who can read, write, and solve arithmetic problems. They believe that good teachers are able to "weave a complex web of connections between themselves, their subjects, and their students so that students can learn to weave a world for themselves" (Palmer, 1997, p. 16).

Common Planning

Turning Points (Carnegie Council on Adolescent Development, 1989) envisions a middle school where validation occurs for every student: "Every student must be able to rely on a small, caring group of adults who work closely with each other to provide coordinated, meaningful, and challenging educational experiences" (p. 37). In an effort to enable diverse learners to be academically successful, cooperative planning among a team of middle level teachers is essential. Stevenson and Erb (1998) reveal that common planning time—among many other elements—is a necessary part of a casual path that leads from the implementation of changes in student grouping procedures and different scheduling techniques to maximize learning, through intermediate outcomes to improved student performance. In fact, they state, "without the common planning time, greater job satisfaction, improved climate, and increased student supports for learning are unlikely to occur" (p. 52).

Seen as a priority, the recommendation for "a common group of teachers with a common group of students and a common planning time is critical" (01). If a team is to function successfully, the core teachers must be in continual communication with one another. It is unrealistic to expect teachers to accomplish a collaborative process such as teaming without the time and opportunities necessary to communicate about their process. Establishing organizational structures that foster teachers' reflections, collaborative planning, and curriculum integration is essential. Developmentally responsive middle level principals address this issue by indicating that their schools are structured so teachers are able to meet everyday with common planning time. Meeting in small groups gives teachers "the facility, the opportunity, for lots of conversation about what is happening in their classrooms" (08). Teachers know students better as a result. They can care for them more adequately, plan and personalize their learning more effectively, and assess and report on their progress more meaningfully. Teachers also know each other better. They can give each other moral support, plan students' programs collaboratively, and share ideas and insights about issues concerning individual students. If used properly, common planning time can be used for dialogue regarding "issues related to the middle school philosophy and the whole adolescent psychology thing" (04). Listen to what else developmentally responsive middle level principals had to say:

> They [the teachers] have double planning. We arranged the schedule so the guidance counselors meet with them [the teachers] once a week. The administrators also meet with the teams once a week, so we can talk about the kids and the curriculum. (09)

> I think the teaming is essential. I don't know how we could operate without it because it gives us an opportunity to communicate about the kids. It gives us an opportunity to communicate with the parents. It gives us an opportunity to almost develop an individual plan for each student. So, I don't know how I could run an effective middle school without it. It's not all about academics here and just what you learn in class. It's about growing and developing. (32)

Personal Qualities (Personality and Understanding)

As active middle school supporters, Doda, George, and McEwin (1987) reflected on the twenty-five year history of middle schools. "What works today has less to do with modern technology and sophisticated curriculum plans than it does with the personality of the teacher and how students experience that teacher on a daily basis" (p. 5). In attempting to explore a definition of expert teachers of young adolescents, Mills (1997) advises, "Middle level administrators must be alert to the qualities called for in effective middle level teachers" (p. 38). The contribution of personality should not be overlooked in this process. Personal qualities often take a prominent role when principals identify a strong candidate among choices for a middle school staff. These are the teachers who meet the students' needs and work well with young adolescent learners. Other principals made very poignant comments regarding the teachers they saw as best suited for middle level learners. They used words like *motivation, flexibility, patience, creativity, sense of humor, respect,* and *a love of children* to describe strong middle level teachers. They stressed what they saw as important:

> I look for the individual to have some type of magnetic personality that you sense is going to bring some excitement to the kids and the classroom. . . . I look for the sparkle in their eyes, for the ability to think with some creative intelligence. Sometimes it's the quiet kind of motivation. (11)

> High energy; the ability to sell the subject—to make it relevant, clear, and interesting to youngsters; . . . teachers who are in the classroom, hallways, at their events. You understand that one day they [students] may love you, and they may dislike you the next for no apparent reason. Even though the prospective middle school teacher may know the subject, you hire them more for their personality than for their subject-matter expertise. . . . Personality characteristics are very, very important for a middle school teacher. (16)

> Patience, development of a professional approach, flexibility, empathy, compassion, love for children, greater understanding of adolescent needs, and adaptability to change. . . . (43)

Caring/Nurturing/Relating

Kohut (1990) stresses that, in quality middle schools, a sense of community and interdependence is present, a commitment to caring relationships is obvious, and a high success rate with young people in all areas is apparent. Several of Maeroff's (1990) comments support Kohut's assertions and point to a caring atmosphere, which in his view, is related to the school's overall success. He notes that a reliance on the quality of human interactions can lead to a sense of community for students and teachers that thrives, where "close bonds are encouraged and competition is discouraged" (p. 507). Maeroff suggests that this supportive atmosphere, with its stress on nurturing, positive, interpersonal relationships, is linked both to teacher commitment and to student achievement in schools. Ashton and Webb (1986) discuss various research efforts that support links between educator's sense of commitment and satisfaction; supportive, collegial interactions among teachers and administrators; opportunities for caring, personal involvement with students; student achievement; and organizational effectiveness. In fact, Beck (1994) is so strong in her conviction to practice a caring ethic in schools that she writes:

> Furthermore, I believe that a conceptual framework that emphasizes personal development, the cultivation of community, and an ethic of caring offers the only valid starting point from which academicians and practitioners can hammer out organizational and instructional theories and methodologies that can adequately meet the challenges facing education. (p. 2)

In addition to imparting knowledge, encouraging problem solving and developing critical thinking skills, developmentally responsive teachers nurture and support their students through the learning process. A study of best teams at best middle schools reinforces the importance of caring teachers. It found that "the most consistent characterization of teachers on the exemplary teams referred to the respect, understanding, and commitment teachers manifest in their relationships with their students (George & Stevenson, 1989, p. 11). Empathy is underscored by Davies (1995) in her outline of the personal qualities needed in the ideal middle level teacher. Davies writes, "The ideal middle level teacher also communicates caring by remembering what it was like to be a 10-to-14-year-old. These memories evoke empathy and empathetic teachers relate more effectively to young people" (p. 157). According to Doda, George, and McEwin (1987), "Effective middle school teachers work to weasel their way into the hearts of the young adolescents they teach" (p. 5). In not underestimating the value of affection in creating bonds, the caring relationship between teacher and student "removes the psychological blocks to learning—insecurity, fear of failure, fear of rejection, alienation from peers and parents, and a thousand other emotional ills to which adolescents are heir (p. 5).

As we already know, the link between caring and learning is very strong. Erb and Stevenson (1999) hold that "when students feel genuinely cared about by the adults in charge of them, they behave themselves and they learn" (p. 66). Research suggests that the pervasiveness of a caring ethos and an empathic regard and respect for students that focuses on individual and interpersonal growth and development can result in measurable, positive outcomes in schools. A sense of loyalty, belonging, and responsibility in the membership can emerge. Students, according to Noddings (1992), will "do things for people they like and trust. . . . They listen to people who matter to them, and to whom they matter. We are reminded by Palmer (1993), "But what scholars now say—and what good teachers have always known—is that real learning does not happen until students are brought into relationship with the teacher, with each other, and with the subject. We cannot learn deeply and well until a community of learning is created in the classroom" (p. xvi). The middle school reform movement is predicated on this belief.

Whether they were familiar with the research or had observed practices that work, developmentally responsive principals commented on the need for advisory and counseling opportunities. A fairly new principal concluded, "Teachers need to be caring, understanding, and empathetic; they need to have the skills to instruct in a classroom setting that makes the best use of students of this age group and their personality types" (12). A caring atmosphere in middle schools offers young adolescents a place where they can feel safe and wanted. Teachers who truly care about students will find a way to help all children succeed.

Principals were concerned about their interactions with teachers and stressed the need to hire what they called "good," student-centered teachers. They talked with enthusiasm of the principal's role as provider of encouragement and motivator of teachers and students. These principals were complimentary and supportive of their teaching staffs, stating that "a good, caring, nurturing teacher who loves kids is just as important as content" (07). They believe that "good things are happening in the classroom" (09) and that "our teachers care about the kids" (14). This same administrator proceeded to list more than a dozen activities throughout the school year specifically designed to heighten collegiality and foster positive relationships. Others demonstrated similar support for teachers who are understanding of their students' growth and maturation process:

> The most important thing is the quality of the relationships—the interactions on a daily basis. It's especially important in middle school because kids don't want to be embarrassed; they don't want to be backed into a corner. The way they're handled in front of their peers is probably the most important thing to them. Teachers need to be sensitive, caring, patient, and respectful. (22)

> Teachers must have a basic understanding of what this age group brings to school and of their social and emotional needs. They need to have a solid content background, want to work with this age group, be a team player, reach out beyond the school day, participate in extra curricular activities, and truly care! (34)

> The teacher has to care about student success and the students in general. If they don't care about students, they shouldn't be in teaching at all but even more so at this particular level. They really have to know a lot about the human growth and development of students at this age and know what it takes to help them succeed. I think they need to be enthusiastic. I think they need a positive attitude because the kids pick up on any negative attitude. And I think they need to be student-centered. (29)

SUMMARY

Overall, the principals in this study focused on teachers and their abilities to positively educate the "whole" student, not just the academic side. They view a "child-centered orientation and real caring concern for kids" (14) as their number one priority in hiring. Principals stressed the need for middle level teachers to be strong in content areas and in the context of teaching the young adolescent; and they expressed support of the active recruitment of teachers who "care, know their subject, and espouse the philosophy that kids are always first in my class" (15). The educational enterprise of acquiring knowledge and of solving problems frequently becomes stressful. Ericksen (1984) observed that, as a result, teachers often fulfill the role of counselor and mentor. He stated: "Teachers appreciate the anxieties, confusions, conflicts, and tensions generated in the academic pressure chamber and are useful sources of information about course routes and career alternatives. Students seek out their teachers as persons whose judgment is respected and whose confidence is trusted as counselor, mentor, and friend" (p. 97). According to developmentally responsive principals, teachers with a commitment to excellence and a positive attitude toward young adolescents are the best teachers for middle schools.

Parents as Partners: A Smorgasbord
of Educational Resources

"A strong parent-school relationship is a valuable resource" (Robbins & Alvy, 1995, p. 207). Developmentally responsive middle level principals recognize that this statement is true in more ways than one. While research documents the numerous theoretical benefits gleaned from parent involvement, chapter 2 anecdotally describes the lived experiences. Seen as ambassadors, coordinators, advocates, and cooperators, parents of middle school students can be involved in a variety of forms, fashions, and functions. Strong leaders are not threatened by their presence, but rather welcome parent contributions. From volunteering to advisory councils to parent education and training sessions, effective middle school principals value the parents of their students and cherish their added help and support. Parents, in turn, are eager to accept meaningful roles and authentic opportunities to aid in their child's learning process.

ACCEPTING AND RECRUITING PARENTS AS PARTNERS

In "viewing parents as partners and not adversaries" (13), developmentally responsive middle level principals acknowledge parents and their presence in more ways than one. While research documents the numerous theoretical and academic benefits gleaned from parent involvement (Brough, 1997; Desimone, 1999; McNeal, 1999), this second theme vividly describes the lived experiences. "Inviting them into the discussion and opening up the process breaks down a lot of barriers between the teachers, the school, and the community" (12). Strong, responsive leaders are not threatened by their presence, but rather welcome parents' contributions. "My motto is, whenever you come, bring a friend" (19).

Willingly Accepting

In outlining their agenda for middle level reform, Williamson and Johnston (1999) declared that "Middle level educators must advocate forcefully for the needs of young adolescents but must also be attentive to the perspective of students and parents as they traverse the system" (p. 16). Keeping this in mind, along with the Carnegie Council's (1989) advice to unite families and schools through "mutual respect, trust, and communication" (p. 36), responsive principals work diligently to engage and reengage families in the educational process. Understanding that parents are usually nervous when their children leave the nurturing environment of the self-contained elementary school for the larger middle school, responsive leaders attempt to alleviate fears by proactively building bridges and accepting parents as partners. They provide guidance about what and how parents can get involved to promote their children's school achievement. They recognize and respect parents' needs to ask questions, clarify expectations and goals, and engage in open discussion with school personnel without being perceived as pushy or unknowledgeable. As one participant succinctly said, "I have a Parent Teacher Organization (PTO) that is incredibly involved, but not intrusive, which is a nice combination" (01). Listen to how much some of the principals recognize the interdependence of parents, student, teachers, and administrators as key to establishing productive partnerships. They clearly value sustained engagement of parents within the school setting:

It is an absolute must. The days of seeing the parent as the enemy is long gone. Parents are our partners. (34)

It's always positive with more parent involvement. We're all working together as a team. The teachers are on the same page as parents, the parents are on the same page as teachers, and everyone's on the same page as the school. Kids know that they can't get away with anything, either academically or socially. So certainly with parents being actively engaged in the school and being partners, that partnership in that sense becomes a true component to the success of the school. (27)

It's been a real positive. Parents here are real good. Even parents who have a tendency to be contentious are pretty intelligent, so there's usually a string of truth in what they're saying. (22)

Actively Recruiting

The need for enhanced and meaningful parent involvement and community connection seems to be among the least controversial areas in public education. However, one challenge facing middle schools is the decreasing parent involvement as students progress from the elementary grades to the middle grades (Epstein, 1995). As a result, part of a comprehensive program of school, family, and community partnerships must include active, systemic recruitment efforts to ensure that all stakeholders are involved. Developmentally responsive middle level principals initiate the unifying process and embrace the opportunities to nurture strong, successful partnerships with individual parents and parent groups. They convey to parents that they are welcome; that their opinions are valued and their concerns are heard; and that school is a safe, respectful, caring environment for them and their children. Great effort is spent reflecting, rethinking, and adapting to promote increased and sustained parent involvement. Interactive dialogue is used as a powerful tool for empowerment, transformation, and the cultivation of a climate of trust.

I try to go after them. I try to recruit. I encourage parents to get involved in all kinds of ways. This is their school. I encourage them any way I can. Every opportunity that I have to . . . in terms of inviting them in emotionally, physically, and intellectually. (31)

I encourage people to come out and to say what is on their minds and how we can do this job better. We are partners in this thing with you and your youngsters . . . anything we can do to bring parents in is extremely important. (23)

I let people look in and walk in. I believe our parents need to feel welcomed and invited, and I take every opportunity to do that. I want parents in; I want them to feel good about what is here. I will listen to their concerns and look to collaborate with them on activities and programs and services. I want them to be an active part of their children's education. (25)

VALUE IN PARENT INVOLVEMENT

Academic Value

A strong and consistent association exists between students' ability to succeed academically and the extent to which they feel that their parents take an interest in and support their academic and personal aspirations. A survey conducted by MetLife (1998) found that "Students who do better academically are more likely than students who have academic difficulties to feel that their parents take an active interest in their school lives, that they provide them with the home support they need to succeed academically, and that they encourage them to pursue their dreams" (p. 3). The research literature overwhelmingly supports parent involvement as a tool to instill the value of education, provide support for success, and participate in the child's education at the middle level (Epstein, 1995). K-12 studies linking parent involvement with a variety of student cognitive and affective outcomes are quite extensive (Cotton & Wikelund, 1989; Desimone, 1999). Well-planned and well-implemented family and community involvement activities have been linked with student achievement and positive outcomes, including increased achievement test results, a decrease in dropout rate, improved attendance, improved student behavior, higher grades, higher grade point average, greater commitment to schoolwork, and improved attitude toward school (NMSA, 2000; Olson, 1990). In fact, recent research (Marjoribanks, 1996) reveals that parent involvement can exert even more influence on students' school success than families socioeconomic status. In this study, middle level administrators appear to be in universal agreement that the involved parent leads to a more successful school–home relationship. They understand that what they do to involve parents makes a difference in how parents—and how many parents—remain involved in their young adolescent's education. In describing such benefits, one participant went as far as to say, "That's what it's all about, 95 percent of students' success is whether or not parents are effectively involved in their education" (19). Others view parents as valuable assets to their schools:

I think our parent involvement is really excellent because our parents care about more than just raising money. They are concerned about grading, programs, and teacher personalities and responsiveness. While they can be challenging, they are certainly involved, intelligent people who care very much about education; and I think we're very fortunate in that. (02)

Our parents who are here on the formal and informal levels are, almost without exception, the parents of children who are in the top ten, or the top twenty, of our classes. (06)

If parents are involved in their child's education and know what's going on, their child generally will be doing better in school. . . . Their kids generally have a better connection to school. Are they always better in achievement? Not necessarily. But I think parents who know what is going on have a better understanding when they ask questions. (15)

Absolutely, let's face it, involved parents reinvolve kids. The more involved parents are in school, the more the school is held accountable. Yes, without question, our most successful kids have the most involved parents. It's not brain surgery. (22)

Social and Emotional Value

One mission of schools is to educate young people; maximize their abilities; and provide them with the knowledge, skills, and ability to develop intellectually. A second mission of schools is to help young people develop physically and emotionally and maintain healthy growth and development. A third mission is to help young people develop socially, as citizens and meaningful contributors to society (National Education Goals Panel, 1998). Researchers have repeatedly found that schooling is as much social—how students relate to each other and to the adults around them—as it is intellectual. Advocates for middle level reform propose that schools need to be responsive to the developmental needs of young adolescents in addition to being academically excellent and socially equitable (National Forum to Accelerate Middle-Grades Reform, 2000). Responsive principals promote this by providing regular opportunities for teachers to interact with students and parents in informal activities that support relationships beyond the academically-oriented relationships of the classroom. Parent involvement increases clarity in communication and allows a firsthand exposure to the middle school culture. "Keeping parents informed, having them feel welcomed and involved" (03) enhances their perspective, corrects miscommunications, and nurtures their support. "We want them to be more involved in the daily routine of the kids . . . that's how they buy into a new program, when they understand it" (11). Middle level principals report that students of involved parents show evidence in varying ways of the value behind and beyond the connection:

> So when you bring the parents in . . . first of all...you break down the miscommunication. And second, they get to see and experience what the school is all about and . . . we have nothing to hide. (05)

> It's clearly documented in all the research that parent involvement in a child's education does not end at sixth grade. Middle school children don't need to see their parents in school all the time to feel good, but they do need them to be involved and feel welcomed coming to school. During middle school, I think students need to feel supported more than ever! (25)

> Now typically at this level kids take on an attitude that is part of their growing up that is difficult to deal with sometimes, especially for the parents. However, if the parents hang in and stay involved, it does make a difference with the kids in the long run; no doubt in my mind. (32)

> Absolutely, when a partnership exists between parents and the school, there is a clear understanding that students' attitudes change. Everyone has the same goals, and students admire and respect the fact that the adults in their life care about them. (34)

CREATIVITY IN PARENT INVOLVEMENT

It is usually during middle school when many young people feel it's "not cool" to be seen with their parents. As a result, when the student enters early adolescence, the parent increasingly loses touch with the school, hence with their education. Although young adolescents want and need greater self-regulation, they also want and need closeness with and support from their parents. The solution seems to lie in giving new and creative definitions to school and community involvement. It demands that the school reexamine its organization and incorporate a wide range of flexible, school-initiated strategies and activities aimed at strengthening the links between home and school. Reaching beyond the traditional PTO, school newsletter, open house, and parent conferences, developmentally responsive leaders provide families with such opportunities to become engaged in different ways at home and school. Believing that parents are more responsive when their children's school calls on them for help, suggested techniques include a "help" solicitation form to be completed by parents. "If you want to help us out, here are the things you can do . . . we get about three or four hundred of these back . . . it gives us a database and that's how we get parents involved" (15). They also suggest that, in an effort to be more inclusive and ensure the success and equity of their school-home partnerships, they be aware of the special needs, concerns, linguistic and educational backgrounds, and work schedules of the families they serve.

The need for parent and community involvement remains indisputable, and the solution calls for innovative solutions. Parents will stand for no less than meaningful involvement. A report from the Office of Educational Research and Improvement (1998) cautioned that no one-size-fits-all practice works when it comes to developing school–home partnerships. With this is mind, educators must be sensitive to the personal and cultural needs of the family and provide opportunities for involvement that meet those needs (Driscoll, 1995; Meier, 1995). According to Burke and Picus (2001), a welcoming school environment that respects community diversity includes orderly facilities, friendly staff members, adequate two-way communication strategies and support services, and a comprehensive volunteer development program. They further recommend scheduling weekend and evening meetings, providing translation services for second-language speakers, offering site-based childcare, securing transportation for meetings, and providing student home visits and telephone calls to students' families for follow-up. Such diversity provides a positive advantage that can nourish the flow of creative ideas, a wide variety of talents, and positive interaction among all stakeholders.

Developmentally responsive middle level principals are increasingly receptive to the value of parent involvement and espouse resourceful approaches that build upon diversity for involvement and engage families in different ways at home and at school. "You do this through a number of vehicles—you bring them into the school, you have newsletters, teams invite them to their meetings, you hold special programs" (23). According to one principal, the cost of failing to acknowledge, value, and welcome parents is exorbitant. "I suspect if we don't have broad family support, or (in turn) broad student accountability to their families, we lose" (10).

Communicating

As noted by NMSA (1995), "Since school achievement is directly related to the degree of family support and involvement in the child's education, systematic, two-way communication with parents and families becomes especially critical" (p. 18). Developmentally responsive middle level leaders agree. They work hard at understanding parents and developing effective, productive relationships with them. "A great degree of communication back and forth with parents" (05) serves as a bridge between the school and home, enables positive and constructive feedback, and yields "cooperation and compliance" (05).

Effective middle school principals provide regular updates in the curriculum, assessment plan, school profiles, and school programs. They inform parents on a regular basis of school activities, student achievement, and other important information. They are intent on keeping parents constantly informed via both traditional communications (i.e., notes, newsletters, meetings, conferences) and some unusual ways that are instructive. For example, positive phone calls to parents build trust and are used strategically. "We established a policy where we are positive and communicative. We have a 24-hour turnaround policy for the return of phone calls" (22). Another example is a parent-information center that includes a reading space, a listening center, an instructive video station, and computer facilities with access to the Internet. Others include techniques such as, "All of our teachers are required to use voice mail to post their homework and messages to parents" (27). Some principals buy space in local newspapers to share school events and report student successes. Whether its through the endorsement of a PTO, monthly newsletter, parent–teacher conferences, interim reports, individualized progress plans, or report cards, the middle school program that collaborates to ensure parents are kept abreast of their child's academic performance enhances broader participation. Developmentally responsive leaders realize the importance of both formal and informal opportunities for the exchange of information and the sharing of expectations:

> It is outstanding. I think that's another hallmark of an effective school by the way parents are connected. We have a parent communication number that is very important. Parents still need to stay connected, so we create opportunities for them to learn more about our program, instruction, and curriculum. (24)

> Well, we have a parent newsletter. We have our Home/School Association speak at the back-to-school night to continue to invite parents. We have a person set up to call for volunteers. And we just continue to talk with them and keep them in touch. We put an announcement on our e-mail site. We have a Web site for the school and the district, and we post our daily announcements so that parents can keep in touch that way, too. (32)

> Communication has been ongoing, in writing, with the notion that adults and children need to work together. I promote it best by letting people know that it's not my school, rather it's our school; and by communicating to them that their child's success is crucial—all working towards the same goal. (34)

Attending

Generally speaking, parent involvement as reflected in attendance at school functions tends to decrease as children move into higher grades. Parents who come to the school to watch and support student performances, sports contests, and other events have an opportunity to meet other teenagers' parents and develop a parent network. They also get a chance to chat with their child's teacher and administrators. These informal conversations reinforce the home–school partnership and nurture the academic success of students. Regardless of the nature of the event, be it an open house, a fund-raiser, teacher conferences, or even a team meeting, parent-friendly events enhance collaboration, communication, and cooperation. Additionally, through attendance at such functions, these parents become "ambassadors" for the school—because they have information they can share and they better understand how the school works. Successful strategies of inviting parents to attend include the following:

> Let parents know we're a team here . . . it's not us and them. This is a community process, a community building. They are part of the team . . . if your child is in the sixth grade, you can sit in a sixth grade level meeting and hear what's going on. (13)

> Parent involvement is totally different at the middle level than it is at the elementary level. First of all, kids don't want their parents to be as involved. They are learning to be independent and, well, they should. They are cutting those apron strings just a bit. They don't want Mom to show up quite as often as they did when they were little. Therefore the need for parent involvement changes. But what often happens is that parents become totally uninvolved, let go of their kids too fast, and don't keep track of them; and it all falls apart without at least some parent involvement. So we try to make different kinds of things so that parents can attend one thing but don't have to come to everything. (32)

Volunteering

Seen as ambassadors, coordinators, advocates, and cooperators, parents of middle-schoolers can be involved in a variety of forms, fashions, and functions that support schools and benefit students. From volunteering to advisory councils to parent education and training sessions, developmentally responsive middle level principals value the parents of their students and cherish their added help. The interviewees "rely on them [parents] as a support" (06) and "our best PR people"

(12). Effective principals actually do "a lot of proactive kinds of things to get parents involved in special activities that are going on either in the building or the district" (04). They use parents' strengths, skills, and interests to improve the school through such activities as: observing, preparing instructional materials, decorating, guest reader, field trip chaperone, classroom activities, parent newsletters, workshop presentations, career education, committee work, tutoring, school programs, clerical work, and extracurricular activities. Parents, in turn, are eager to accept meaningful roles and authentic opportunities to aid in their child's learning process. They are interested in sharing their expertise and time to assist students and teachers. Aware of the "correlation between parent involvement and educational achievement" (07), they simply want to know how to help they can help their child.

> When I ask for volunteers, I have more than I can use. The parents here work real hard for the kids and if you need something, you can get them galvanized and energized. (22)

> From day one I've let parents know that we're a team here. It's not us and them. This is a community process, a community building. They are part of the team. I've encouraged them. Our parents come in and serve as moderators and speakers for real world activities. (14)

> Our home and school association works very well together. They not only are involved with fundraising, but also work as tutors in the school, volunteers in the library, chaperones for activities, and pretty much anything you need. (23)

While research corroborates the fact that volunteers can help schools and students reach important goals, developmentally responsive middle level leaders advise schools to plan accordingly. Burke (2001) recommends that principals of middle schools support the organization, training, and purposeful assignment of volunteers by: recruiting widely to increase the number of volunteers, involve diverse families, and extend the skills and talents available to assist the school and students; preparing volunteers with targeted training so that their efforts are effective; and preparing teachers to work well with volunteers.

Decision Making

According to Hoover-Dempsey and Sandler (1997), and a number of other researchers (Epstein, 1995; Sanders, 1996), parent involvement makes a difference in helping children succeed. However, including parents in various aspects of school governance necessitates a lot of discussion along with a sense of parental self-efficacy, clear role descriptions, and expectations and opportunities from the school. "This requires schools to engage parents early in the middle school experience to the underlying philosophy and rationale for effective middle level schools and ensure that they know these best practices are grounded in research and professional experiences" (Mulhall, Mertens, & Flowers, 2001, p. 60).

In addition to keeping parents informed about school policy changes, effective schools often include parents on committees that oversee school policies. Parents need to know that they have the right and the responsibility to contribute their ideas and share in the leadership and decision-making processes within the schools. As a result, responsive middle level leaders involve parents in the development of parent guidelines, parent associations, advisory committees, school improvement or school site councils, school programs, and activities. Many schools use a PTA or PTO as a forum for parents to give input in decisions and policymaking. Such organizations act as formal avenues for engaging parents in dialogue, offering parental perspectives, and voicing parents' expectations and concerns, which can then lead to systemic change. Developmentally responsive middle level leaders encourage their parents to attend such meetings and share opinions and insights on school-related matters.

> We run an active parent organization, leave the door open for communication, offer a wealth of parent education opportunities, and try to help parent organizations see their roles as decision makers and not just cookie bakers and fund-raisers—it's a constant ongoing pattern of strategies to help promote on a day-to-day basis the role of parents as equal members and not unwanted visitors. (33)

> I promote involvement by just being myself; being open; answering questions; and asking the parent advisory committees for input, advice, suggestions, etc. (36)

Educating and Advocating

Many of the participating middle school principals reported that their parent organizations offered workshops to other parents on relevant topics such as family literacy, parenting, communication skills, child development, academic standards, and life-long learning. Advocacy groups monitor schools or work for school improvement by promoting both parent involvement and community involvement in interagency executive and policy boards, community mentoring programs, and decision-making processes. Such insights provide a base for renewed dialogue among all of the educational stakeholders and a clear understanding of the wealth of knowledge that parents have to offer. They advocate for their children's best educational interests by standing up for their children, arranging for tutoring, teaching, helping others to learn, seeking out resources, and keeping abreast of school events and occurrences. They also ensure two-way sharing of educational information relevant to students.

> I think there is a direct relationship to people who are positively invested in their youngster's education and are truly concerned about making the school a better place by providing whatever expertise they have. . . . Some of them are very, very organized and very academic. Our PTO sponsors, plans, and coordinates young writer's day, career awareness day, family fun nights, and the parent advisory committee; volunteers; chaperones; tutors; helps the store, book fair, and library workers; etc. (01)

> At our PTA meetings, we got away from just having a business meeting. We started to theme every meeting where we had a guest speaker come in and talk about a subject specific to middle school level needs, and that attracted parents. They wanted to hear about adolescents, drug use, language arts, and what the national math standards are for middle schools. That really connected them into the school and helped a lot. (07)

> Our parent group has been very helpful; they have been active politically and have pushed the board to get things done. They've done a marvelous job. In the last two years, the board has grown to listen to them—kind of like the squeaky wheel gets the grease in this case, and that's how politics work I guess. They have been great advocates for our kids and our school. (29)

SUMMARY

Referencing the work of the National Network of Partnership Schools, Sanders and Simon (1999) conclude that when middle schools develop comprehensive programs of school, family, and community partnerships, they can involve the families of early adolescents in many ways that are developmentally appropriate and can improve the quality and outreach of their programs from year to year. "Through interactive dialogue, each member of the school community can be acknowledged and valued for his or her unique and noteworthy strengths and talents. Hence the goal of promoting sustained parent involvement is to, ultimately, provide for high-quality, developmentally appropriate educational opportunities that foster school success for all students" (Causey & Wood, 2000, p. 48).

The Triple A's of "Success for All and Every Student:" Adjust, Adapt, and Accommodate

"Ensure success for every student through the elimination of tracking by achievement level and promotion of cooperative learning, flexibility in arranging instructional time, and adequate resources (time, space, equipment, and materials) for teachers" (Carnegie Council on Adolescent Development, 1989, p. 9). Chapter 3 relays the thoughts and reflections of middle school principals as they knead and tweak this recommendation from *Turning Points*. Candid comments about inclusion, special education, differentiated instruction, diversified strategies, and I.D.E.A. are included. The overarching theme that emerges is the significance of an optimistic, dedicated commitment to the "success for all and every student." Developmentally responsive middle level leaders live and instill a "can-do" attitude; they hold high expectations and find a way to make things work as nothing is too hard or impossible. Realizing that all children want to believe in themselves as successful people, effective principals espouse the theory that success breeds success. "Absolutely, if you don't believe in success for all you better get another job" (24). Responsive principals enjoy problem solving with people and do not hesitate to adjust, adapt, and accommodate where necessary. Their mode of response is grounded in what is best for their students. They value excellence and equity for all!

SUCCESS FOR ALL AND EVERY STUDENT?

Theme three relays the thoughts and reflections of developmentally responsive middle level principals as they knead and tweak *Turning*

Points' (Carnegie Council on Adolescent Development, 1989) recommendation to "ensure success for every student" and *Turning Points 2000's* (Jackson & Davis, 2000) recommendation to "ensure success for every student." Candid comments about inclusion, special education, differentiated instruction, diversified strategies, and I.D.E.A. are included. Philosophically, they believe that "kids ought to be in the swing of things as a normal part of our program, in the least restrictive environment" (22). The overarching theme that emerges is the significance of an optimistic, dedicated commitment to the success for all and every student. "We have to do everything we can to meet the needs of the kids" (13), including "getting outside of the box . . . trying things in a different way" (06), and "mainstreaming as much as possible" (15). This sense of inclusion enables students with special needs to gain from working and teaming with their middle level peers, while providing every student with valuable lessons in working effectively with others.

Hough and Irvin (1997) remind researchers, "At the crux of the entire middle grades reform movement will remain the crucial issue of student achievement relative to middle school programs, policies, and practices" (p. 351). Developmentally responsive middle level leaders are acutely aware of this, bluntly stating "if the kid fails, we fail" (14). Recognizing that "the period of life from ages 10 to 15 represents for many young people their last best chance to choose a path toward productive and fulfilling lives" (Carnegie Council on Adolescent Development, 1989, p. 20), effective principals tend to aim high, expect much, and trust that their students will prosper as a result. "Success for All and Success for Every Student" is their underlying belief. "Absolutely. All students, if given quality instruction and a fair chance to achieve, will achieve" (17). Simply put, improving student achievement is their number one priority!

> Yes, ALL kids can learn; ALL kids can improve. ALL students can achieve at high levels. ALL students can succeed; ALL students can get from point A to point B. The object is to have a goal and make sure you do whatever you can to get that kid there. (04)

> I firmly believe that kids will aspire to exactly the standard you set for them. If you supply them with the support that they need and you have

teachers who are motivated to get things done, it's amazing what you can do . . . absolutely amazing. (07)

I think that all students can succeed whether they are elementary, middle, or high school. It just depends on how you reach them and what you do to work with them. I want my teachers and staff to always think that all students can succeed and find a way for that to happen. (32)

HIGH EXPECTATIONS!

Jackson and Davis (2000) argue, "The most critical feature of a healthy middle grades school environment is equally high expectations for all students" (p. 175). Developmentally responsive middle level schools adopt high expectations and are characterized by strong adult–student relationships; an environment that provides opportunities for every student to excel; and programs and practices that help young people grow up healthy, caring, and responsible. *This We Believe* (NMSA, 1995) states that as young adolescents are quick to sense, educators "convey their expectations by their own examples, as well as by gestures, remarks, and overall attitudes" (p. 15). Educators who set high standards are considered to be caring and supportive. And, for some students, having high standards says that teachers care enough about them to be tough with them and to expect the best from them. "Such confidence promotes positive attitudes and behaviors and serves as motivation for students to achieve" (NMSA, 1995, p. 15). In the process, valuable lessons are learned.

Research by Lumsden (1994) supports the premise that the nature of the expectations educators hold for students exerts a powerful influence on achievement. The fact that developmentally responsive middle level principals set and communicate high standards is a crucial aspect in helping their students meet achievement criteria. Such leaders live and instill a can-do attitude; they hold high expectations and find a way to make things work as nothing is too hard or impossible. They use a wide variety of activities and symbols to communicate motivational goals, accepting that visible symbols illustrate and confirm what is considered to be important in the school.

Motivation and Success

Expectations for success are transmitted through the relationships a student has with adults and peers. When students care about what others think about them and expect from them, they feel a personal stake in meeting those expectations (Arhar, 1992). Conversely, students who feel that no one knows or cares what they are capable of doing, who believe that they are viewed by others as incapable of high-level achievement, will lower their expectations of themselves to "fit" what they sense is the prevailing view of their own incompetence (Kramer, 1992, p. 29). The relationships established within the middle school affect both the quality of student learning and the quality of teaching. "A positive atmosphere where teachers want to come to work, where they feel good about what they do, and where students have success" (35) can be created by developmentally responsive principals. When teachers have the opportunity to know students well, when they are involved deeply and personally with students on a daily basis, they are more likely to make the kind of intense investment in their students—the tailoring and targeting of teaching strategies to students' interests and learning needs—that fosters greater student achievement (George & Alexander, 1993). In turn, as teachers become more effective in helping a broader range of students learn, student motivation increases, creating a "win–win" upward spiral toward improved student performance (Eccles & Wigfield, 1997; Erb & Stevenson, 1999).

> All kids can succeed no matter what. I don't think there is one lesson plan for any one class. I think there are multiple lesson plans, multiple strategies, cooperative education, lecture, use of technology—all of these can help a youngster succeed but nothing can help a youngster succeed more than high expectations from the classroom teacher. (23)

> There is such an atmosphere of achievement in this district that the pressure is self-imposed. Test scores in this building have been high for the last five years. If those scores drop, I find it somewhat personally embarrassing. Whether or not I have control over this factor, I internalize that stuff, so I work really hard to keep the expectations high so people know that those things are valued. (22)

You have to define success. Your goal has to be that every kid who walks through your doors is going to get a fair shake and is going to do well academically. I mean, why would we expect anything less? You want all your kids to be successful. But success doesn't mean that you're going to be successful in spite of performance. True esteem is a result of genuine, meaningful accomplishment. I don't go for watered-down coursework. I think we need to be real rigorous! (12)

Students' achievement can be positively affected by public acknowledgements (Renchler, 1992). Frequent recognition and vocal praise for doing something positive can motivate students to do well. Staging academic awards assemblies, giving trophies for academic success, displaying awards in trophy cases, and publicizing successes can help students see that the desire to be successful academically is recognized and appreciated. Most exemplary middle schools report that they emphasize public acknowledgement of student achievement by praising students for academic success and positive student behaviors and by recognizing appropriate and success-oriented student actions. The desire of developmentally responsive principals is "to leave a legacy of excellence, a reputation for running an excellent school, a school dedicated to learning" (31).

Can-Do Attitude

Leadership begins with the belief system of the leaders followed by deliberate study, development, and implementation of a responsive educational program that strategically aligns curriculum, instruction, learning tools, assessment, and staff development that is focused on the needs of students and teachers. According to one respondent, "Our middle school philosophy is 'setting kids up for success.' We involve all kids and look for ways to address their needs" (36). Leaders who believe similarly that all students can succeed have a good chance of helping students reach their fullest potential. It takes patience, perseverance, and prioritizing. "You maintain high standards and find ways for all kids to meet them" (12). Developmentally responsive middle level leaders maximize and improve student achievement by believing in their students and in their students' capacity to learn, grow, and improve. The depth of their commitment and determination can be seen in the actions they take. What they say, how they spend their time, and how they allocate resources make measurable differences.

> You have to have the willingness, the forthrightness, and the desire to fight for what you believe in. You need some realistic leadership qualities like the ability to use power in a constructive way, the ability to understand the environment (political and community) of how your school is operating, and be able to deal with other constituencies and be proactive in decision making and problem solving, see the big picture. (19)

> Eighty percent of our students are on free and reduced lunch . . . two thirds are minority . . . one out of six is special education or bilingual. So, you know, we have a lot of needy students. And we give the entire package to all the students. We're proud of that. We serve the kids who need support. And we try to have the enrichment and accelerated activities and opportunities for the kids who can excel. (04)

> I'm a strong supporter of inclusion. After graduation all these students are going to be recruited into our society, and they can make a contribution. They are intelligent; they can make contributions. Why do we put them off in little corners? They have learning needs, emotional needs, and a lot of other different needs; but they can be met in the classroom. They can be addressed in the classroom with the right kind of support and a curriculum that will meet their ability. I'm a strong supporter of "where there's a will, there's a way!" (29)

ADJUST, ADAPT, ACCOMMODATE!

As reminded by Carpenter and Anglin (2000), "Schooling that fails academically fails absolutely" (p. 43); developmentally responsive middle level principals face the dual task of both motivating students toward high achievement and supporting students who fail to meet the standards. This responsibility underlines the importance of truly understanding and helping all students through the transitions of their young adolescent lives. For this to occur, Roney (2000) suggests that middle level leaders first need to recognize the challenges of this age, specifically, the developmental and physical changes through which their middle school students proceed. She explains that "from this recognition of adolescents flows an understanding that is embodied in flexible and creative teachers willing to adapt and work off the strength of their students" (Roney, 2000, p. 228).

Lipsitz (1984) agrees and found that the most striking feature of successful schools was their willingness and ability to adapt all school practices to students' individual differences in cognitive, biological, and social maturation. Developmentally responsive principals enjoy problem solving with teachers, students, and parents; and they do not hesitate to adjust, adapt, and accommodate where necessary, "making everyone feel important as individuals but also part of the whole" (02). They "identify the individual differences of the kids and are able to modify their programs and the curriculum to meet those individual differences" (15). Their mode of response is grounded in what is best for their students, providing the attention and support when and where necessary, recognizing that "it looks different for every child" (14). Responsive leadership values "diversity learning" (14), excellence, and equity for all.

Adjust

Being adaptable and flexible in responding to the individual differences in the students is a key ingredient of exemplary middle schools and a key component of developmentally responsive principals' philosophy. "I believe that good teaching is good teaching. I believe that you are the professional and that you adjust and modify your teaching talents to meet the students' needs" (34). To ensure the success of every student, instructional practice must address learners with diverse levels of readiness, rates of learning, preferred learning styles, experiences, interests, and cultural backgrounds. And, to work effectively with such diversity, teachers and administrators need "a broad range of approaches to enable students in a heterogeneous classroom to excel" (Jackson & Davis, 2000, p. 175). According to one interviewee, "The first quality that I look for in middle level teachers is that they are empowered on their own, that they take initiative on their own. They look at the kids' needs and then they adjust their teaching to whatever those needs are" (32).

Utopian middle level teachers "willingly modify curriculum and instruction to meet the needs of students" (Arth, Lounsbury, McEwin, & Swaim, 1995, p. 18). Because middle school students' learning styles are in flux as they develop new ways of thinking and learning, labeling a preferred style at one time as a characteristic of a student is limiting and possibly dangerous. According to Epstein and Salinas (1992), "promising programs for students who need extra help in the middle grades use a variety of visual, auditory, and manipulative materials to teach and reinforce skills but do not pigeonhole students in a single or fixed learning style" (p. 290). Responsive principals agree, "If we need to alter the curriculum based on individual students' needs, then we do. Sometimes with just minor adaptations, students can be successful" (12). Such diversity is a hallmark of middle level learners. Middle schoolers range from child-like to adult-like, from socially awkward to socially adept, from emotionally insecure to brimming with confidence, and from concrete to abstract in thinking—sometimes seemingly all in the same student on the same day (Tomlinson, Moon, & Callahan, 1998). Cognizant of this, developmentally responsive middle level leaders give their teachers the flexibility and autonomy to create the most efficient learning environment for each student in their group. They encourage them to "teach the same standards and the same content but at different rates using different approaches" (21).

It's the job of the teachers to fine-tune and adjust to the level of the students in the class. Even within that, there are differences that must be addressed. You can't treat every child in the same way. So that curriculum has to be fine-tuned and adapted to meet the needs, the special needs of each child in the class. (04)

I do believe that we make every effort to generate opportunities for success for all by our insistence on effort and commitment to being as creative and as talented as we can in our strategies. We want kids to do their best. There is a real attempt to put everyone in a situation where the barriers to their success are removed. (25)

I think we make the adaptations possible. Our teachers are aware of the students' IEPs or 504s. They are required to review them and to try to as-

sist the child in any way they can. We modify our curriculum and modify our instructional models to be able to best meet the students' needs.
(27)

Accommodate

Because "success is defined differently for different kids" and because "there are varying degrees of success" (35), developmentally responsive middle level principals feel the need "to be able to offer kids
something different, something more accommodating" (20). Lawton
(1993) emphasizes that the "key to middle level instruction involves
exact attention to basics combined with creative variety in the overall
presentation" (p. 9). Responsive leaders are aware of this and advocate
for a wide variety of developmentally appropriate instructional strategies. They encourage their teachers to adapt curriculum and instruction
to the developmental needs of their students, to use varied activities and
materials, to ask varied questions, and to promote thinking. They understand that effective teachers are aware of genuine gains for each student and that "the effective teacher adjusts, remediates, enriches, and
develops future plans based on examination of evaluation results"
(Lawton, p. 10). For this to realistically happen, Arth, Lounsbury,
McEwin, and Swaim (1995) state that "middle level teachers must have
both the professional knowledge and the personal initiative to alter
their teaching practices to fit the needs of their students (p. 18). The in-
terventions of developmentally responsive principals are supportive of
this notion. The want to see teachers "inserviced and retooled to give
kids what is needed" (31) and are willing to become "students of their
students" (Tomlinson, 1999, p. 2) in the process.

> If middle schools truly do address the needs of early adolescents, then
> our teachers and our administrators have to be trained to deal with this
> age group ... certainly our teachers have to understand what those needs
> are and tailor curriculum and instruction to their students' needs. (01)

> We need a genuine concern for students as people, concern for their ac-
> ademic progress, and an openness to changing the plan if it is not work-
> ing. It means being able to take a risk to do something different with that

kid, a willingness to make accommodations and adaptations, to get out of the box so we're not teaching the same old way, and to really connect kids with the learning. (06)

I think teachers ought to be made aware of multiple ways to deliver instruction. They ought to be taught how to recognize when you need to reteach in a different way to teach kids that are not understanding. They ought to be taught the various modes and models of teaching middle school kids. (31)

SUMMARY

Data collected from this study indicate that leadership responsive to the needs of students involves an understanding of, and an appreciation for, the intellectual, physical, psychological, social, moral, and ethical characteristics of young adolescents. As a result, developmentally responsive principals purposely design their school programs, policies, curriculum, and procedures to reflect the needs and characteristics of their students. They believe in success for all and every student and work diligently to establish a learning environment that honors both the cognitive and affective domains of education and growth. In the process, they promote the development of relationships between adults and students, seeking the support of parents and community members as true partners in the endeavor of educating today's young adolescents.

Responsiveness to Faculty and Staff

And the Walls Came Crumbling Down: A Unified Profession of Administrators and Teachers

"In these new post-industrial educational organizations, there are important shifts in roles, relationships, and responsibilities: traditional patterns of relationships are more flexible, leadership is connected to competence for needed tasks rather than to formal position, and independence and isolation are replaced by cooperative work" (Murphy, 1999, p. 3). Chapter 4 introduces the developmentally responsive middle school principal as a partner in this collaborative attempt to improve schools for students. Principals recognize the need for the bureaucratic walls of administrative construction to crumble and give way to professional autonomy, teacher efficacy, and supportive environments that enhance commitment and expertise. Through open doors, open ears, open mouths, open minds, and open hearts, middle school principals are able to effectively build the necessary support for change. They are present and available, they listen attentively, they communicate appreciation and support, they collaborate and share decision making, and above all, they obviously enjoy what they are doing. The positive characteristics of these middle school leaders pave the way for the walls of division to crumble and the call for a unified profession to strengthen.

A CALL TO UNIFY

Discussing postindustrial educational organizations and the changes that have occurred, Murphy (1999) wrote:

73

. . .there are important shifts in roles, relationships, and responsibilities: traditional patterns of relationship are altered, authority flows are less hierarchical, role definitions are both more general and more flexible, leadership is connected to competence for needed tasks rather than to formal position, and independence and isolation are replaced by cooperative work. (p. 3)

Most of the middle level principals who participated in this study recognize these shifts. As exemplified by the words of one of the respondents, they understand the need to "break the organizational structure that through the years fostered teacher and administrator isolation" (11). They want to unify the profession, "flatten the hierarchy," increase empowerment, and encourage professional interdependence over professional autonomy. "I ask them to do it because I want them to do what works for them. They're dealing with the kids. They know on a day-to-day basis what works best" (32).

Developmentally responsive middle level principals view leadership as a shared responsibility transferred among the participants. They recognize and want to foster leadership in others. They strive for cooperation and respect within the faculty and between the faculty and themselves realizing that "the old model of a principal saying 'this is what we're going to do and how we're going to do it' is not really effective" (14). According to those interviewed, nurturing relationships means making connections, convening for celebration and nourishment, and finding opportunities to collaborate and network around common goals.

The collegiality aspect of it, I think we return that to this building because generally everybody in this building is here for the same reason, and that is to educate kids . . . focusing on teaching kids. That brings everyone together as a group and as a family. (05)

I believe in a lot of involvement . . . you have to be really respectful of the culture and the traditions. Team organization lends itself, I think, to empowerment because they're kind of self-led. They (teacher teams) take care of their discipline, they take care of their kids, and they make decisions for their team, so right there you have a different mind-set. (11)

The teacher empowerment is important. When I first came here everybody had to go through the principal to get anything done, whereas I'd much rather get a lot of people involved and let them make the decisions because it's our decision, not my decision to make. I've given them the autonomy to make their own decisions. (29)

However, also evidenced from a number of the principals' comments is the fact that the road to deconstructing the traditional, centralized control of top-down structures for decision making is not always easy. The reality is that some teachers become set in their ways and comfortable with their roles. Some of the middle level principals spoke candidly about the "walls that commonly exist between most teachers and administrators" (09) and how teachers prefer these walls of division to remain. The principals admit that "working on a learning organization that will be self-led" (11) is no simple task. Listen to how they struggle with the recommendation from the Carnegie Task Force on Teaching as a Profession (1986) to replace hierarchical structures with networks and collaborative partnerships for decision making.

It was amazing how there was a clear line of delineation . . . here's the teacher, here's the administration. That was ingrained in a lot of our teachers for a very long time, and they trusted and felt good with that. I had to build trust . . . be good to my word . . . take risks . . . and understand that failure is just another step toward success. (07)

I very much believe in a democratic process and in building leadership in everyone, and that we're all partners here. That has not been the climate of this school for a long time, so it's going to take a little while. I think people feel more comfortable with their role as teacher, having someone else be the administrator. My goal eventually is for everyone to work as partners, as colleagues—not you're the principal; you're the assistant principal. Rather, what's the next thing we're going to deal with together? I think that's the best way. (08)

I try to allow teachers in the decision-making process as much as possible . . . I think the climate is a positive climate. And I try to have a feeling that there is a collegial relationship, not teachers here and administrators there. That's not always easy to do. It's a tough part of the job to make up because with some people, no matter how hard you try to have collegial relationships, they'll want that wall there for whatever reason. (04)

OPEN DOORS—PRESENT AND AVAILABLE

While collegial relationships fostered by collaboration help to break down barriers among teachers and administrators, intellectual discourse that promotes feelings of unity and commonality is also needed. "Strong instructional leader principals are seen as visionaries who are out and around. Their presence is created by day-to-day behavior that is consistent with their values" (Smith & Andrews, 1989, p. 36). Developmentally responsive middle level principals are emotionally invested; they regularly tour their buildings, "communicate effectively" (03), contribute to meetings, and attend school functions. They are "very visible in the building . . . trying to present a motivated energetic image to students and teachers . . . attending common planning meetings on a regular basis and following up to make sure things are happening" (04). In the words of one principal, "You have to be emotionally part of what they're doing to expect emotion out of them. People need to see you involved in the process. It makes a big difference" (14). The middle level principals who participated in this study agree and recognize the need to open their office doors, to transition from a managerial focus to an instructional focus, and to develop the skills necessary for team building (Trimble & Miller, 1996). They work hard at making their presence felt and at making themselves available. Succinctly put, one respondent said, "Open door, open door, open door. One of the things that I changed when I came here is that the decisions used to be made in this office. I have tried to empower the teachers as much as possible" (06). Many others concurred:

My door is open except when I'm meeting with somebody privately. I'm approachable. I'm out in the hallways. I meet the students. I greet the teachers. (29)

The decision-making process is one of consensus building. I always say that I run my building with an open door. (15)

Instructional leadership is being visible around the school, getting in the classrooms . . . it is allowing your staff to know that your first and foremost job is the improvement and achievement of the school. In terms of communication, I guess that speaks for itself. Through the team meetings, faculty meetings, my curricular resource people . . . and even though it's an overused term, the door is always open. (13)

According to Smith and Andrews (1989), "As a visible presence, the principal interacts with staff and students in classrooms and hallways, attends grade-level and departmental meetings, and strikes up spontaneous conversations with teachers. The principal's presence is felt throughout the school as the keeper of the vision" (p. 18). Making themselves accessible to the staff, making their presence felt often by moving around the building, and making an effort to actively participate in school activities are overlapping elements of positive school climates and effective, visible principals (Iannaccone & Jamgochian, 1985). Bulach, Boothe, and Pickett (1997) agree. In their recent study investigating shortcomings of school leaders, 15 categories of mistakes were identified. Mistakes subsumed under the category of poor human-relations skills occurred most often, including a lack of trust, an uncaring attitude, failure to circulate with staff, and staying distant. The majority of the participants in this study recognize this behavioral flaw and, as a result, they ". . .try to get out and walk through the school building and talk, try to go to team meetings, meet with team leaders. [They] try to have good, real open relationships . . . the doors are always open" (06). Another principal felt that "part of my job is to make sure I'm pretty much out there and communicating . . . selling the things that need to be sold" (04).

More than half of this study's participants reported that middle level principals should constantly display behaviors that reinforce school values. Developmentally responsive middle level leaders believe that it is important to know on a firsthand basis what is going on daily in the school. "I think visibility is the key. I make a commitment to get into every classroom every day. I am usually able to do that. It might only be 30 seconds, but the kids are very comfortable and familiar with me being in the classroom and the hallway" (22). They strive to make it possible, through an open door policy, for others to express both personal and professional matters, and to manage time to be out–and–about and available during school hours. "We meet regularly, both formally and informally. I think they feel very comfortable coming in the door and just sitting down and asking to talk" (12). Listen to the salient thoughts of other middle level principals on this matter:

It takes time to build . . . I've always had an open relationship, the doors are always open, you don't need an appointment—we're a team. (11)

I try to meet with teachers informally; my door is always open. My door is open, you don't need an appointment. (09)

We are very open. The office is always open; I'm always accessible. I like to deal on a personal up-front basis . . . and I hope and I feel that everyone in this building is comfortable to come to me and I come to them. The doors are open, everyone is welcome, and we try to get everyone to feel good. (05)

OPEN EARS—ACTIVE LISTENING

Being accessible is one thing, building the trust needed for the walls of division between administrators and teachers to crumble is another. In the study by Bulach et al. (1997), the second most frequently occurring mistake made by principals deals with a category of behavior labeled "poor interpersonal communication skills." The example most frequently given for this type of mistake was the failure to listen, doing paperwork, and not maintaining eye contact. Behaviors illustrative of failure to listen were often interpreted and perceived as signs of not caring. Clark (1995) stated that it takes effort and sincerity to be a leader who is capable of sharing and listening to the voices of teachers when creating dreams for their schools. Successful principals, according to Blase and Blase (1994), build trusting environments by encouraging openness, facilitating effective communication, and modeling understanding. Simply put, "You have to bring the people in, open the sharing. You have to listen to alternatives, then build consensus" (10). Many of the interviewees believe that they listen with respect, always striving to truly understand the other's point of view.

If a teacher wants to come in and tell me what they think or what their concerns are, I'll take the time to listen to them. If I'm going down the hall and somebody says, "I need to talk to you," I'll say, "Do you have the time right now?" and we'll do it right there. (15)

I think the qualities needed to be effective are in those intangible things around interpersonal skills, communication skills, and the willingness to listen and take a lot of input. (04)

You need to listen to people and give them avenues to express their opinions. You have to create mechanisms for them to do that . . . have to listen to all. I try to be an open door principal where kids can come in and express their concerns. (19)

In a school with a strong sense of community, teachers and administrators feel valued and know that their opinions, ideas, and backgrounds contribute to the school as a whole. They recognize not only their own importance, but also that of everyone else in the school. As one informant stated, "There are other things we can benefit from—the thoughts, the beliefs, the backgrounds, and the experiences of others. You bring them into the conversation and you allow them to make a decision" (12).

According to Hoy and Sabo (1998), "The principal in an open climate listens and is receptive to teacher ideas, gives genuine and frequent praise, and respects the competence of their faculty" (p. 127). Many of the interviewees for this study recognize that active listening requires one to attend to the person who is speaking and to hear what is intended. "They are happy for somebody who is listening to what they want to do and what they want to try" (06). Listening, caring, and trusting are interrelated. Listening conveys a caring attitude, and caring is a building block for creating trust (Bulach, 1993). Many effective middle level principals accomplish this by providing forums for the open exchange of professional ideas and research. Note how several of the middle level principals talk about listening attentively, responding appropriately, and encouraging regularly:

Having that time for people to dialogue is important and necessary . . . time to share strategies that are working with the kids. Just having time to have a conversation. I think there are little things you do that foster that collegiality from the fact that people know that you listen to them. I've never made a faculty meeting agenda myself, they've always come from the people. (11)

I'm trying to learn to listen better, because I think that the best way to bring about change is to listen to what everyone is saying and where there is a need for change. You listen, you meet as a group, and then you make a decision. (02)

Listening, hearing things carefully, understanding the emotion that comes behind the message, and being able to articulate clearly are all critical aspects of effective leadership. (33)

OPEN MOUTHS—BUILDING A POSITIVE SCHOOL CLIMATE

If increased student achievement is the ultimate goal, then establishing and maintaining a positive school climate is vital (Speck, 1999). Once teachers and administrators acknowledge that they value a collaborative work culture—that they want to work *together* to help all students learn—then they can create a learning environment, focused on outcomes, that offers higher potentials for student achievement. According to *This We Believe* (NMSA, 1995), "The climate of a developmentally responsive middle level school is safe, inviting, and caring; it promotes a sense of community and encourages learning" (p. 18). Generally speaking, the principals involved in this research recognize this connection, value human relationships as paramount, and celebrate positive risk-taking. Some feel that their main role is "to be there for their teachers and to support them" (16). In their willingness to tear down the walls of division and open their doors to listen, they recognize the need to be proactive in their appreciation and support of their teachers.

The number one priority of a principal is to always appreciate your staff. If you appreciate your staff, recognize accomplishments, stay on top of the literature, and always be proactive rather than reactive in your capacity, then I think a principal is fairly intact. (13)

If somebody comes to me with a good idea, my response is, "Just go for it." And I'll try to generate support in groups . . . I'll give people a lot of flexibility. If I think it's a good idea I'll say, "Go for it!" But I really try and encourage people to take risks. (04)

When maintaining a positive school climate, DeBruyn (1996) stated, "There is a law of management called the Law of Positive Reinforcement, and it states: 'In the absence of positive reinforcement from appointed leaders, negative human attitudes and behaviors are most likely to emerge from the group being lead'" (p. 1). Quite a few of the middle level principals interviewed for this study appear to have consciously or subconsciously grasped the true spirit of this law. They report themselves as "communicating praise verbally and through informal written notes, cognizant that good communication fosters mutual understanding" (44). They assert that their visible presence as rewarder is most keenly felt when they give positive attention to staff and student accomplishments. They are aware of the need to compliment, motivate, and communicate in ways that build positive relationships with all. Acknowledging the achievements of others is a regular practice by principals who are strong instructional leaders (Giammetteo & Giammetteo, 1981). The following respondent agrees:

We have very good communication; not only between faculty and administration but also between my custodians, cafeteria workers, and support people. I recognize and support them as I do my faculty members. So, we do a lot of things together. There's a lot of collegiality; we get together for special times in the year. And, I always try to recognize any staff member who has done something outstanding, no matter how big or small. (13)

According to Payne, Conroy, and Racine (1998), middle schools that maintain high staff morale manifest four key elements: communication, recognition, opportunities for growth, and shared leadership. According to several of the participants in this study, the developmentally responsive middle school principal should be able to assemble, develop, and maintain a staff of dedicated educators who are able to understand the unique characteristics of young adolescents and work with them. They see it as their responsibility to motivate staff members to become involved in the school culture. They believe that they help to facilitate collaborative efforts in meeting school goals and improving instructional quality. They recognize and value the contributions of all. According to Blase and Blase (1994), effective school leaders model a high level of professional talk. Most of the interviewees noted that the purpose of this professional talk is to encourage others to be actively engaged in middle school theory, thought, and philosophy. As principals they see themselves as inviting others to share ideas and materials, ask big questions, make presentations, engage in joint planning, and conduct research. The following remarks outline their desire to inspire group purpose, provide contingent rewards, and increase teacher efficacy (Hipp, 1996):

> Teachers feel good about working with the kids. I think we've made some changes in terms of staff morale and they feel good . . . their efforts are appreciated. And I'm not sure that's always been the case here. So I let the ideas bubble up and then we encourage the ideas as they come up. "Can we do this?" . . . "Sure we can!" . . . "How do you want to do it?" (06)

> I try to empower teachers who have new ideas, people who have the initiative to try something new and have the energy and enthusiasm to do that. There are all sorts of opportunities for give and take. . . . I give them written feedback if I need to. There are a lot of lines of communication. (04)

OPEN MINDS—BEING RESPONSIVE

According to Williamson and Johnston (1999), "The continued success of middle school education depends upon responding to current challenges, engaging in thoughtful and reflective discussion, and not continuing reliance on a checklist or menu of programs" (p. 11). For real responsiveness to occur, Williamson and Johnston believe that the proponents of middle level education must actively and openly embrace the revision and refinement of programs so that the issues confronted by contemporary middle level schools may be addressed. In order for this to occur, principals need to be open to a variety of strategies and suggestions. They also need to be open to input from a variety of stakeholders.

Schools that manage change best, asserts Fullan (1999), are those with a collaborative work culture. "They develop a collaborative work culture as they become professional learning communities, go 'wider' by connecting with the external environment, and go 'deeper' by taking time to explore the fundamental values and purposes of education" (p. 1). Keefe, Valentine, Clark, and Irvin (1994) found that effective principals are more skilled in staff relations and involve more faculty and a broader array of persons in the planning and decision-making processes. Principals who take a democratic approach to leadership trust their teachers with important decisions. Based upon self-reporting, they "invite others into the conversation" (12), provide their teachers with a high degree of autonomy, share their teachers' concerns of meeting the needs of students, and "are willing to live with what the group or committee decides" (12). Others felt similiarly:

> To be up-front and honest and explain the advantage of change and get the people that are going to have to experience the change on board. The strategy I use is to explain to them where we should be and how we should get there and encourage them to come on board and let them make a lot of the decisions in the changing process. And when they make those decisions, they buy into it. Anytime you get into something that involves change, you get some kind of resistance. But if you get the people involved in making the changes, it goes a lot easier. (16)

> My nature is I will talk toward a consensus. I've had discussions with parents, and I've had discussions with staff. There really is consensus building. I firmly believe in empowering the teachers to make a decision. I think you have to get as many people as possible to buy into it. (15)

Whitaker and Valentine (1993) found that the more effective principals and their teachers share a common perspective about teachers' input into the decision-making practices, particularly the degree of teacher involvement. Striking that balance between the principal's administrative responsibility and the teachers' democratic collaboration is not an easy task for professionals today. "It's tough to bring change to a veteran staff. They're perfectly happy, and they don't want their world changed" (15). Other principals verbalized similar sentiments, claiming that "making decisions together, and not in isolation" (11) takes political savvy.

I like having everything happen down below. If I have an idea, I really spend some quality time having the staff go over it, and then we come to a consensus whether we're going to do it or not. (14)

There are other things that we can work on collaboratively to get things done. You can't run an organization with 70 people with just one way of doing things. If everything's collaborative, you'll be viewed as "wishee washee," and you're giving away all your power and you really have no authority base. If you do everything in an authoritative fashion, it goes against what middle schools are all about. So there is a balance. (07)

Along similar lines, Spindler and George (1984) noted an essential role of middle school principals, "Principals must be a good moderator for open meetings, where divergent thinking must be expressed or recognized while working towards consensus" (p. 294). Several of the principals interviewed for this study commented that they do in fact use a consensus dialogue; they "will talk about things with the staff and parents, and try to reach a consensus" (15).

People truly do think differently. What is so obvious to me is not obvious to others. And what I think is a logical and good solution to a problem may be viewed entirely differently by someone else. And, although that sounds trite, just to understand that the person sitting across the desk may live an entirely different reality, perceive things differently, view things differently, unless you understand their motivations and their thought processes, you get nowhere. So, I think the second piece of those listening skills is absolutely critical. By nature, as administrators, we're problem solvers. We want to solve problems. We want to make everything right for everybody. But, in order to do that effectively, you've got to really keep your mouth shut. Avoid the tendency to formulate your response before a person is even finished. (22)

Working with colleagues, examining student work, developing rubrics, looking at data, reading professional literature, identifying problems, and designing possible solutions are all part of the daily process. Many of the participants describe some of the strategies they use to create such high levels of involvement and collaboration in problem solving, governance, staff development, team operations, and decision making. Developmentally responsive leaders view themselves as willing to "give great latitude to people that come with great ideas," and they like "teachers being energetic and enthusiastic" (04). They also describe the perceived effects of their efforts in terms of community, trust, empowerment, growth, and shared expertise. Smith and Scott (1990) reported that involvement also leads to enhanced relationships between teachers and administrators and higher employee satisfaction. These findings and the words quoted pave the way for the walls of division to crumble and the call for a unified profession to strengthen:

> I think that our people work real well together. We communicate. We involve everyone in the decision . . . people are risk takers. They're not fearful that they're going to get hammered if things don't work the right way. We have a good enough relationship that we can talk to each other, and if things aren't happening, we can talk about it without feeling threatened, and people respond favorably. (03)

> I like collaboration . . . if people are not invested in something, it's not going to happen when the classroom door closes. So I think that the general strategy that I use is to try to develop consensus and be able to compromise. And sometimes it means that you take small steps or it takes you longer to get there; but ultimately when you get there, you're where you want to be. (01)

OPEN HEARTS—A PASSION FOR THE MIDDLE SCHOOL

Clark and Clark (1989) identified 12 desired characteristics of leaders attempting to bring about middle level reform. A passion for middle level education, a concern for the well-being of all persons in the school, and a good self-concept were among the qualities listed. The middle school principal should not be someone who sees the middle school principalship as a stepping stone to the high school principalship, but instead as an individual who feels a sense of commitment and bonding with young adolescents and the faculty dedicated to serving this population (Valentine, Clark, Irvin, Keefe, & Melton, 1981). When asked how they felt when they were appointed as a middle school principal, most of the respondents in this study were excited, "anticipating it with a lot of enthusiasm" (05). "I'm happy to be here and I want the teachers to feel good too. I want them feeling positive about coming to work everyday" (06). Many of the principals identified a passion within themselves to work with young adolescents and to help create emotionally safe school climates and developmentally responsive schools for them. "I sort of always keep in mind that the kids come first . . . the overriding mission is to do the best thing you can for the kids" (15). Others agreed:

> I was excited. The whole philosophy of the middle school appealed to me. I feel very comfortable with this age group of kids. I do a lot of community coaching with youngsters this age, and I teach Sunday school to sixth graders. So, I felt right at home. I was really excited. (06)

> They (middle school teachers) realize this is a pretty nice environment. And even the people are different in middle school. The staff is friendlier. They're more people-centered. On Fridays we have breakfast for the whole staff and people take turns every Friday to provide breakfast. Things are just a little kinder and gentler. (14)

Meaningful leadership values the human soul and spirit. It is hopeful, empathetic, and a source of inspiration to others; "it reconnects the heart and mind" (14). Almost all of the middle level principals who were interviewed view their role as that of an inspirational leader, a human resource developer, and a change agent (Williamson, 1991). Being positive, cheerful, and encouraging; doing things with teachers; and involving the staff in expressing and setting their own goals are overlapping elements in positive school climates and effective, visible principals (Iannaccone & Jamgochian, 1985). Those interviewed for this study comprehend the importance "of being visible, friendly, and outgoing . . . of trying to present a motivated energetic image" (04). In a building where a positive school climate exists, there is a feeling of warmth. Students, staff, and visitors feel welcome; and teachers feel empowered. Everyone involved feels good about themselves and their contributions to the larger community. It is evident from the research that collaborative environments increase job satisfaction, help reduce conflict, reduce stress and burnout, and raise morale and trust for school leaders (Shedd & Bacharach, 1991). The vast majority of the interviewees agree that open hearts are necessary:

I think you're all buying into the same train ride and they (the teachers) want to make sure you're on board. They want to make sure that you understand what they're going through as a team to get to resolution. You're involved in the process sometimes. . . you have to be emotionally part of what they're doing to expect emotion out of them. (14)

Qualities? A sense of humor. . . Not to take yourself too seriously. . . and a deep-seated belief in what you're doing and why you're doing it, and communicating that to your staff. I have a great respect for our staff here. I'm always recognizing the staff and making sure that they know they are appreciated. (13)

The other piece is equally balanced in all that we do: we treat each other with dignity and respect, whether you're administrator to teacher, teacher to teacher, teacher to student, or student to student. We foster a relationship among all stakeholders that values the individual person. (25)

SUMMARY: A CALL FOR UNIFICATION

From its beginnings as a response to the rising clerical needs of schools (Cotton & Savard, 1980), the role of school administrator has evolved over time (Beck & Murphy, 1993). This evolution has taken us on a journey that characterized the principal as a strong, forceful leader who administered the school from the top down, to an empowering principal who facilitates and relinquishes control for decision making (Short & Greer, 1997). During the early stages of this developmental process of role definition, the division between teachers and administrators into "two distinct camps with a minimum of linking elements" (Murphy, 1999, p. 2) occurred. In other words, the walls of division were constructed. This chapter argues that these lines of demarcation have outlived their usefulness; the time for a unified profession has arrived.

The middle level principals who participated in this study recognized the problems posed by this division and have issued a clarion call for the walls of division between teachers and school administrators to crumble. Through open doors, open ears, open mouths, open minds, and open hearts, these principals are able to begin the process of building a new foundation for educational administration that will hopefully result in the improvement of the quality of life and learning in schools. For school administrators, this new foundation involves being present and available, listening attentively, communicating appreciation and support, collaborating and sharing decision making, understanding the nature of the students who are served and their needs, and enjoying what they do. Developmentally responsive leaders recognize the importance of reuniting the professions of teaching and school administration and refocusing their attention on the core technology of schooling—the processes of teaching and learning. As one of the middle level principals stated:

> Instructional leadership is being visible around the school, getting in the classrooms. It is allowing your staff to know your first and most important job, which is the improvement and achievement of the school. Leadership is a combination of things. It's your knowledge of the curriculum; it's your relationship with your staff. It's bringing the parents into the fold and letting your kids know you're interested in them and their achievements. It's having the initiative to put new programs on the table and then see if they're fully implemented and evaluated. It's bringing in the community and letting the community know that the school is a good place. (13)

As evidenced by the interview data presented in this chapter, important shifts in roles, relationships, and responsibilities are occurring in schools. These role shifts are happening at a time when social constructivist views of teaching and learning and issues related to school choice are taking center stage in school reform. Traditional patterns of relationships between teachers and administrators have become more flexible with leadership connected to competence for needed tasks rather than to formal position; and independence and isolation have been replaced by cooperative, collegial work.

The operant goal is no longer maintenance of the organizational infrastructure but rather the development of human resources and learning organizations (Speck, 1999) aimed at school improvement. And as the school improvement literature (Saphier & King, 1985) indicates, teachers and administrators must work together for the greatest results to occur. This joining of forces should be characterized by trust, care, high expectations, experimentation, appreciation, open and honest communication, and the protection of what is important in the life of the school.

In short, following the advice of Murphy (1999), it is time to rebuild the field of educational administration with a pedagogical scaffolding that will allow us to truly focus on the work of schools—teaching and learning. It's time for the walls between administrators and teachers to crumble.

Lifelong Learners: Job Shadowing and Peer Modeling for Teachers and Administrators Alike

"Principals are responsible for teaching (not telling) teachers to become better teachers, parents to become better teammates in their child's learning, students to become better learners, district office personnel to become better colleagues in the educational enterprise, and citizens to become better supporters of education" (Hunter & Morrison, 1978, p. 11). Given these responsibilities, and the desire to escape the ever-present danger of professional obsolescence, developmentally responsive middle level principals view themselves as lifelong learners. Chapter 5 highlights their emphasis on differentiated professional growth options for teachers, as well as for themselves—the lead teacher.

Effective principals encourage visits to other classrooms and schools, want their faculty to observe great teachers up close and personal, and believe in the benefits of long-term internships for future administrators. They give more credence to experimental learning versus university training, they participate in appropriate professional development activities throughout their careers, and they support peer modeling and job shadowing wholeheartedly. In the words of one of the respondents, "We're (administrative team) participating in the educational process with them, growing with them, getting involved in their activities" (14).

DIFFERENTIATED PROFESSIONAL DEVELOPMENT FOR TEACHERS

Acknowledging that "theory and practice are just coming together to produce solid information to reform education in the middle grades" (p.

44), Killion and Hirsh (1998) write that the time is ripe for improvement in middle level instruction. Given the short supply of middle school specialists, middle level administrators' decisions regarding professional and staff development may benefit from the advice of Killion and Hirsh: "The most effective and efficient way to increase their numbers is through high-quality, comprehensive staff development geared specifically to middle-grades instruction " (p. 44).

While recognizing that there is no one best way to promote staff development, this fifth theme highlights responsive middle level leaders' emphasis on differentiated professional growth options for their teachers, as well as for themselves. They understand the "need to refresh themselves continually" (08) and to "be trained to deal with this age group" (01). They feel strongly that teachers should have a tremendous amount of input into staff development. Encouraging an "attitude of improvement" (22) and "supporting them in their efforts" requires "visibility and some coaching and collaboration" (25). The answer, according to one principal, is "putting people in charge of their own learning and goal setting" (24). Another principal recommends "focusing the professional development on the needs of the kids, not on what the teachers are doing wrong. Put it in terms of students and stress the impact it will have on the students" (44). All of this needs buy-in and direct application. Within the professional development there needs to be a connection to the teacher, and the teacher needs to see it as a needed change.

Self-Analysis and Professional Dialogue

Developmentally responsive middle level leaders encourage their teachers to "engage in professional dialogue with other teachers and become lifelong learners" (20). They agree with Wolfe (1998) that "we need to give teachers time to reflect on their practice, to engage in substantive dialogue with others about what they are accomplishing and why, and to assist teachers in carefully studying new research and innovations to determine whether they validate their practice, require them to rethink their practice, or both" (p. 64). Given the strengths and weaknesses of teacher preparation programs, nothing compares to on-the-job experiences as the best teacher. In fact, the recent California model for retaining new teachers is a "reflective assessment process based on the premise that teachers learn good practices over several years of study, through consultation with experienced colleagues, and by using reflective practice beyond academic preparation" (Lucas, 1999, p. 45). This model gives teachers time to test what they have developed and, with the help of their support providers, they can experience success and failure through the process. This notion of self-reflection is highly touted by the principals interviewed for this study:

> Teachers learn more from their colleagues than they do through professional staff development. Teachers have to see themselves as lifelong learners. You can't meet the needs for your profession in four years of college and no more. Schools have an obligation to provide training within the system and to create environments where teachers view themselves as professionals and want to keep learning and growing and improving over time. (33)

> I think you have to take a step back. I mean you can put a model program in place and you can have all the bells and whistles and the latest jargon; but if you don't have a group of people who are committed to working with kids and improving themselves, then none of this stuff makes sense. (22)

Johnston and Markle (1986) advocate that middle school teachers should reflect together in order to meet the needs of their students. "Teachers must have the opportunity to discuss their teaching with other professionals in a nonevaluative setting. This means that groups of teachers should meet for the expressed purpose of talking about their teaching" (p. 7). Delgado (1999) advocates that "the two most practical ways experienced teachers can help new teachers are through chance meetings in the hallways and through scheduled discussions during common preparation times" (p. 27). By focusing on fulfilling fundamental emotional needs for relationships, Rogers and Renard (1999) hold that what works for teachers also works for students: "When our psychological needs are met, we want to perform to the best of our ability in order to experience positive feelings" (p. 34). Such collaboration with other teachers facilitates communication, enhances satisfaction, and nurtures the desire to grow professionally. Other benefits also include a support system among teachers that encourages innovation and the provision for professional autonomy and decision making about instructional and organizational issues (Clark & Clark, 1987). This type of teacher empowerment appears to take root in gradual steps that set the stage for even more professional growth:

> Empower teachers as much as possible. We have school improvement planning groups now. Every teacher is on it . . . get them to see that they do have the power to change their class, team, and school; then go from there. I don't think I've said "no" to a teacher-generated project this year. (06)

Job Shadowing and Peer Modeling

With such a wealth of experiences and knowledge available, the participants in this study agree with Lawton's (1993) advice to "provide opportunities for the teachers to visit other middle level schools and attend inservice sessions to gain new ideas, reinforcement, and support of transition programs" (p. 3), as well as ample opportunities to "see how master teachers handle the complex issues and situations that inevitably occur during the course of a school day" (Conrad, 1992, p. 17). Time spent observing colleagues, either informally among grade partners or formally with mentors, is crucial to the development of characteristics effective in working with young adolescents.

When discussing differentiated development, responsive leaders believe that teachers "should be able to come to a middle school position where they already are and move ahead. Teachers are at different levels; we shouldn't expect that everybody coming into it is at the same level" (02). They also hold that "teachers need time off from their classes to watch other teachers in action" (07), opportunities "to see other classrooms and observe teaching in a non-threatening way" (35). Such ongoing opportunities to share their unique knowledge bases allow many teachers to explore new ideas and content areas, and to expand their professional skill repertoires. Realizing this, the principals interviewed encourage visits to other classes and schools, want their faculty to observe great teachers up close and personal, and support "peer modeling and job shadowing" (15) wholeheartedly. They like the professional activities that "allow teachers to get out, visit, and experi-ence what other successful middle level programs are doing . . . to ac-tually see things in action" (04). The value of professional develop-ment, in various formats, is consistently endorsed by responsive principals—so long as the focus is upon meaningful application and in-put by those involved. "We learn by doing. I seek opportunities for all teachers to go out and experience as much as they can" (08). This phi-losophy concurs with that of Willis (1999), who states that the peer re-view process makes sense because "no one knows the difference be-tween good teaching and bad teaching better then the best teachers themselves" (p. 5). Listen to other participants' comments about the importance of alternatives and the benefit of realistic settings:

> You can bring all the experts in that you want, you can have people go to workshops, you can have them go to conferences, you can involve them in training, but what is most likely to effect change is to see something new or something different done effectively by one of your colleagues. So, I would say peer modeling and peer coaching is the very best way. In fact, that's one of the things that has led to our relative success in this building. (01)

> I think in-services are absolutely critical . . .if it's a one-shot deal, and there's no other follow-up, then it's going to be lost. Seek opportunities for all teachers to go out and experience as much as they can. It's com-plicated; we need time to interact around progress. When teachers see other teachers experiencing success in the same type of demographic arena, that is the best motivation for them to pursue it. I think a lot of the best professional development gives teachers time to work together . . . be able to think about what they are doing. (15)

> We used to do all types of workshops and teachers sat there and they lis-tened and they heard, but they didn't experience it. I found that the best thing we did with teachers is get them out into the model middle schools and let them see what it looks like. When teachers see other teachers ex-periencing success, that is the best motivation for them to pursue it . . . to intrinsically take it upon themselves instead of an extrinsic kind of in-fluence. (07)

According to Roney (2000) and the participants of this study, forming critical relationships is key to middle level education. These relationships include teachers connecting with teachers in the classroom next door, as well as district-wide colleagues meeting at local and national conferences. Developmentally responsive principals recognize this and provide ways for teachers to create professional connections, engage in reflective dialogue, give each other feedback on their work, and hold each other accountable. Their call for more time corroborates what the Carnegie Council on Adolescent Development (1989) outlines in *Turning Points.* "Teachers need time during the school day to work out schedules and make adjustments in the daily program. They need time to express ideas, talk about students for whom they share responsibility, describe their successes to other teachers, and seek counsel from colleagues on solving problems" (p. 55). Through self-analysis, professional dialogue, job shadowing, and peer modeling, developmentally responsive middle level leaders believe they can help their teachers acquire the characteristics needed in order to be effective in working with young adolescents.

DIFFERENTIATED PROFESSIONAL DEVELOPMENT FOR PRINCIPALS

Internships for Future Administrators

Developmentally responsive middle level principals believe in the benefits of long-term internships for *future* administrators. They see a need to "model more what we do with student teachers where principal interns actually go in and take an active role and maybe, at some point in time, be given the building for several weeks. That kind of on-the-job training is irreplaceable" (01). They give more credence to experiential learning, problem solving, "talking with other principals" (06), and "real world experiences" (08), versus university training. "It's very difficult to learn unless you're immersed in it. So in some way you have to see the model in action. I think to read a book or take a course in it and not be involved in it is very difficult" (14). Others agree:

I think they should have to do an intern period of at least six weeks in a middle school. I really think that you can't learn this job from a book, you have to be in the job, and nobody really understands that until they've spent some time. (02)

I think part of an administrative experience at the graduate level should be an internship at all levels, so that you can get the feel for what a true middle school is. (07)

Programs aimed at final preparation of people for the principalship require shadowing a principal for six weeks, but even that's not enough. It needs to be a year. (19)

There could be no harm done by making it mandatory that you spend so much time of an internship shadowing and being in a middle school. (24)

Mentoring Future Administrators

Practicing middle school principals are asking for "more time to just sit and share . . . dialogue, ask questions, interact" (15) with preservice administrators.

I think a mentoring situation for new administrators is critical. I think any opportunity for discussion and time to be with other administrators to review what you're doing and what others do is always helpful. (08)

Provide direct contact with practicing administrators, provide opportunities to problem solve together, put aspiring principals in schools, assign mentors that will, in essence, provide them with firsthand knowledge of what is going on in schools . . . hands-on and active involvement with issues instead of just textbook questions. (34)

In *today's* schools, the principal's role has become increasingly more complex and arduous. Dealing with competing expectations and the dilemmas inherent in simultaneously managing and leading make supervising instruction, being accessible, delegating, accepting responsibility, and so on, very difficult challenges. According to Butterfield and

Muse (1993), "these changes and demands have been caused by growing legal interpretations, effective schooling research, legislative enact-
ments, increased demands for accountability, the revolution in classroom technology and expectations for site-based management and
restructuring" (p. 4). Consequently, several of today's educational
leaders, who received certification or licensure several years ago, are
simply not prepared for these new demands; they lack the skills and
knowledge required to meet the needs dictated by restructuring and reform. Middle level leaders are not exempt from this trend (i.e., 80 percent of this study's participants received their administrative degree in
the 1970s and 1980s). They are charged with molding exemplary middle school characteristics into meaningful experiences and programs
designed to enhance the social, emotional, physical, moral, and intellectual growth of young adolescents; but they often lack the preparation
necessary to do so. As a result, it has become clear that middle school
principals need to continually update their knowledge base in order to
understand and facilitate the process of change and to develop the
depth of human relations skills required to successfully enhance student learning—the ultimate purpose of professional development.

Many of the principals interviewed for this study are aware of the
substantial changes in their roles; but they wonder *what, where,* and
how they will learn what they need to know to effectively lead their
school communities. The updated literature begins to outline what they
should do, but it does not suggest how or where they will learn to do
these things. Where and how will they learn to create a shared vision,
foster collaborative and team relationships among staff members, allocate resources, provide the information that teachers need to be successful with young adolescents, and promote teacher development? As
Payzant and Gardner (1994) noted, "strong collaborative and instructional skills have replaced strong bureaucratic skills as important qualities needed for effective school principals" (p. 11). Principals, once
trained to be managers, are now expected to be leaders assuming new
roles and responsibilities. In light of this, the practicing middle level
principals in this study were asked to consider *what* they now want and
need to learn, *where* they want to learn it, and *how* they will learn it
best. A description of the professional development activities necessary
to enhance their capacity for leadership follows.

What Do Practicing Middle Level Principals Want and Need to Learn?

Shifting conditions and new images under which schools and principals operate require new skills and new learning. In attempting to understand and adapt to the effects of their changing role, we asked the principals to identify areas in which they lack knowledge, understanding, or strategies for dealing with the changes. By analyzing the transcriptions, we discovered that the principals were clear and consistent about what they needed to learn to forward the middle school reform agenda. In particular, principals spoke about needing further knowledge and skill in the following areas: (1) creating a respectful, collaborative, collegial school culture; (2) understanding, implementing, and assessing newly proposed approaches to teaching and learning at the middle school level; and (3) remaining current (i.e., up-to-date) organizationally, legally, financially, and technologically. These three common areas are articulated below with an explanation of what the principals meant when they talked about these essential areas.

1) How to nurture collegial and collaborative learning environments. Site-based curriculum development and the empowerment of teachers are focusing attention on school culture (Barth, 1988), and the necessity for collegial and collaborative work environments is being highlighted (Fullan & Hargreaves, 1991; Sarason, 1990). Many of the middle level principals seem aware of this and are seeking information that relates to staff collegiality, cooperative efforts, participatory decision making, and attitudes toward change and professional growth. They recognize that the traditional managerial role of independence and isolation is incongruent with the middle school philosophy aimed at creating interdependence. Principals know the task at hand, but they want to know *how* to accomplish the task. How do you get people talking *to* rather than *at* each other? How do you identify the power of existing cultures, knowledge, and role relationships that may impede or support change? How do middle level principals interact with teachers, parents, other community members, and students, and actually engage *all* as a cohesive unit that works toward the school's vision, goals, and objectives?

Middle level principals want to develop strategies with which to accomplish goals and assess progress toward involving others in decision making so that all can learn the collaborative process. They need insight into their natural approaches to interacting with people because, as many of these principals explain, nurturing collegial and collaborative learning environments is not easy. As two participants stated:

> We need some realistic leadership qualities like the ability to utilize power in a constructive way . . . like being able to accurately assess the culture and climate of a building and the political ramifications that impact it . . . the ability to understand the environment (political, community) of how your school is operating and be able to deal with other constituencies and be proactive in decision making and problem solving . . . see the big picture. We need to learn resourcefulness, vision, and how to reach out and create collaborative partnerships with businesses, communities, families, and universities, to find other funding through grant writing. (18)

> A necessary component of professional development would be skills and strategies for creating working relationships between teams and teachers. You know, you are asking adults who primarily have spent their life independently to form teams and collaborate among five or six of them. We need a course on team building and pulling together staff of different backgrounds, interests, motivation, and characteristics to form good working relationships. (25)

[Note: 80 percent of this study's participants are implementing teaming, 83 percent are implementing interdisciplinary teaching, and 59 percent are implementing flexible block scheduling.]

2) How to implement and assess new instructional methods and strategies. To meet ever-changing instructional challenges, a systematic lifelong exposure to instructional methods and strategies is very important. Most of the principals in our sample realize this and desire additional knowledge and skill in the area of program implementation and assessment. Some report that they are unfamiliar with the pedagogy and curriculum that their teachers are implementing as part of middle school reform, and they want and need to know more. They are asking for professional development in the new approaches to teaching and learning so that they can then assess the potential value of programs that they might adopt. Once new teaching reforms are underway, more than half of the principals interviewed stated that they need new knowledge about assessment in order to monitor the implementation and understand whether the reforms are effective. They describe their commitment to actually use the information gained from professional development for classroom application and improvement of instruction:

> I think we need constant staff development on the latest instructional skills . . . cooperative learning, looping, special education rules and regulations, strategies in dealing with kids with different discipline issues, Individual Educational Plans, and differentiated instruction would certainly be high on my list for professional development for administrators. (23)

> Principals of the past were more managers and coaches with excellent interpersonal skills, but they did not need to know or did not know curriculum. Today, principals need to know the curriculum due to the pressure of accountability. (37)

> You never stop learning. I think we need continued interest and education in current practice. You can get stuck very quickly unless you keep up with what's happening. . . . So, we need to continue to learn, to continue to have that energy and enthusiasm for the instructional side. (07)

This concern led principals to a related middle school concept in which they reported needing new knowledge and skill—adolescent development and psychology (i.e., only 41 percent of this study's participants have had any formal middle level training). They advise that more research be done on "what successful middle schools are doing in terms of scheduling, classroom management, cooperative learning, inquiry groups, and really meeting the needs of their adolescent students" (35). Others concur:

> We need more information on the psychology of the middle school student . . . on teaming, scheduling, patience, and understanding of the needs of each student. We need more technology, drug and gang awareness, middle school philosophy stuff, and things related to kids' developmental issues. (38)

We need to have a strong instructional background and need to know and understand adolescent psychology and development. (41)

Design courses that have more hands-on types of learning experiences and what the curriculum in middle schools should look like, what the teaching strategies should look like, what adolescent development is like at that level, how to work with teachers at all levels, veteran and new, types of scheduling and rostering and understanding the needs of the middle level kids. (20)

There is definitely not any instruction [specifically] for middle school administrators. There needs to be some distinction according to grade levels. The administrators need some instruction in the different levels—emotional, social, and academic . . . philosophies are different for different grade levels. What is the middle school philosophy? (39)

3) How to remain current organizationally, legally, financially, and technologically. In addition to their instructional duties, middle level principals today are expected to take responsibility for school improvement planning and reporting; school-based budgeting and financial management; appointment, development, and evaluation of staff; as well as establishment of and cooperation with school advisory councils, crisis management teams, and district level solicitors. Knowledge of the latest technology, experience with various middle school scheduling configurations, and a thorough grasp of the special education regulations are just expected. Cafeteria, boiler room, and air quality inspections are now part of the daily routine. When asked specifically what they need and are currently not getting by way of professional development, practicing middle level principals identified the following areas:

Technology. Being able to stay with the times and find ways to bring technology into the school. Use of technology as a tool as we grow and change, use of teleconferencing with other schools, electronic monitoring activities, distance learning opportunities for staff . . . How to use technology as a tool for the administrative concerns? How to incorporate technology as an instructional tool? How to integrate technology with content? How to get students to use technology for research purposes and for generating reports and multimedia projects? (21)

I see curriculum getting to be more technical again, so keeping current is essential. Distance learning is going to change how we teach, how we deliver materials, and how we address materials that kids have learned. You need to always review, evaluate, and stay current. (32)

Law and Finance. More up-to-date school law, special education regulations, balance between being an educational leader and manager, and dealing with legalities and budgeting. We need more hands-on practice with school finance, school law, curriculum and instruction, teaming, personnel, organizational issues, and disaggregating test data. (25)

More with practical applications of the budget . . . how to plan, how to figure, what can and can't be maneuvered, what needs to be spent by when, etc. (04)

Facilities and Safety. Inservice, wow, could be really dynamic. There is so much that we need. The whole realm of violence in society has changed and there is a desperate need for administrators to learn not only about how to avoid it, but also all the safety issues that have come into your facilities as a whole. I'd like to look at other buildings and see how they are handling the safety issues. (32)

The second thing is dealing with facilities. I was never trained to deal with asbestos, boiler room problems, break-ins, leaking toilets, etc. It's a big challenge just to keep the building running. (18)

Facilities management . . . when I came to be principal I had no clue what the boiler room did, what it takes to maintain a building, or how much it costs for repairs. You have to be aware of the outside things that people don't even think about like the light poles, the electricity, the telephone lines, the cable things for computer networking. I had no idea what you need to check for daily when you go into your building just so that you can have a safe learning environment that is suitable for kids. (42)

Synopsis: What do middle level principals want and need to learn? The principals interviewed in our study are learning to lead middle schools that often challenge existing ideas about school organization; technological advancements; diverse climates; and teaching, learning, curriculum and assessment. To do so, principals find themselves needing a new set of strategies and skills to forward the reforms and bring along their teachers and communities. Professional development can help them acquire new techniques and identify additional issues, themes, and areas for training. Having stressed the content of what principals want and need to know, we now turn to a discussion of where they may or may *not* learn the new information.

Where Do Practicing Middle Level Principals Learn?

According to Seller (1993), professional development in the field of education has traditionally been narrowly interpreted. "If the professional development was an ongoing activity, it meant that the educator was enrolled in a university program and attended a series of courses. Other professional development activities were usually a series of events, most often guest speakers and workshops, which were, at best, loosely connected by a theme or subject focus" (p. 22). More specifically, Barth (1986) contended that professional development for principals has been a 'wasteland.' "Principals take assorted courses at universities, attend episodic inservice activities within their school systems, and struggle to elevate professional literature to the top of the pile of papers on their desks. Many attend, few succumb, fewer learn" (p. 156).

Consequently, district inservice and university coursework have left many principals unsatisfied and unprepared. They find it hard to believe that professional development will ever be engaging let alone helpful to them in running their schools. The reality is that many middle level principals must rely to a great extent on "on-the-job training" for their most effective professional development. Components of effective inservices are scarce in district-based staff development programs for principals, often highlighting only the managerial side of the principal's role, if at all. Some of the principals report a lack of professional development opportunities offered at the district, state, and national levels:

Does it [inservice training for middle level principals] exist in this district? I don't think it does . . . there needs to be some follow-up after initial preparation. (20)

You run into a problem with that. Improving the training of middle level principals usually doesn't happen. There's an assumption that's wrong. The assumption is that because principals hold administrative positions, they already know what they need to know, so the districts don't bother to train them. They just let them go. They've been very helpful in developing programs for teachers but there've been very few in terms of programs for administrators. . . . There isn't much out there for middle school principals to go to. I'm not getting the interaction with other administrators, locally or regionally, at the same level that would be helpful to me. I'm not receiving as much as I should. (31)

I feel that my needs are not being met. They [professional organizations] don't help; I help myself. They send pamphlets, magazines, or short brochures with information. But if you don't read it, you don't learn. If you read it and don't understand it, you don't learn. So, even if they provide information, they don't help you grow as a person. They do nothing to help you grow as a person. They have memberships across the United States, and they have offices and so forth, but they spread themselves too thin . . . they are not able to walk into a district and inservice principals. (27)

[Note: 66 percent of this study's participants belong to NASSP, 56 percent are members of ASCD, and only 36 percent belong to NMSA.]

Fortunately, Seller (1993) states that the range of professional development activities is now being expanded to include not only the traditional activities, but also practices that support collegiality and cooperation. For impact to occur, ideas gained from speakers, workshops, or articles must by examined within the school context. Most of the principals in our sample realize the importance of finding the time to attend workshops, seminars, and national conventions in order to upgrade their skills and rejuvenate themselves. Because none (0 percent) of the middle level administrators in this study have specific middle level certification, they are asking for their professional development needs to be assessed and addressed. They would like to see more cohesiveness and less fragmentation in their development. The principals are asking for more in-house offerings combined with the necessary incentives for them to pursue the required professional development through graduate coursework and active participation in national, state, and regional middle level association-sponsored programs.

I belong to ASCD, NASSP, NMSA, the local Middle School Association, Phi Delta Kappa. I believe they bring me valuable current information, collegiality, opportunities to do presentations and hear other presentations, opportunities to expose my staff, national exposure to best practices . . . validates what we do. (18)

It's important to belong to the organizations. They keep me abreast of what's going on in the field, the latest research being done. The articles are helpful, very timely . . . helps me keep in touch with the middle school philosophy and changes. Also gives me a network. I wish we did more, like get together with other middle school principals in the area four or five times a year. We could form a middle level consortium and develop our own little agenda about what we need to improve ourselves. (29)

First of all, the leadership in the school district has to assess and determine the needs of the existing middle school principals . . . some kind of way, either through a survey, questionnaire of some kind, or by onsite observations and then bring in or prepare inservices in the areas that need to be shored up in terms of administrative skills . . . for example, writing and communication skills. (03)

By taking advantage of going to conferences, getting new ideas to implement, reading their publications (if you have time). I go to hear people talk about how they handle situations similar to mine. We need more regional conferences . . . more could go if they were closer in proximity. Local conferences are easier to get to and not as expensive as opposed to the national conferences that are difficult to get to and expensive. (10)

How Do Practicing Middle Level Principals Learn Best?

Having identified some of the content (what) and professional organizational (where) needs of middle level principals today, we now turn to a discussion of the structures and pedagogical strategies (how) that might maximize principals' learning. Our purpose was to identify aspects of principal professional development activities that seem more or less useful for middle level principals engaged in reform. Having experienced a wide variety of formal and informal inservice opportunities, the practicing principals were in a position to assess their own learning, provide insight into what assisted them, and report the ways that were most beneficial in helping them with their work.

Based on the interviews and the literature surrounding professional development, we were able to identify four components of how developmentally responsive middle level principals learn best. The methods that have the most potential to support continuous professional growth include: (1) identification of needs and involvement in planning; (2) reflection within the school context and sharing with other colleagues; (3) systematic development supported by district time, money, and resources; and (4) competent instructors using practical, adult learning processes. All four characteristics address the necessity for relevant and practical learning opportunities designed to meet the professional needs of middle level administrators.

1) Identification of needs and involvement in planning. In order to foster directly applicable knowledge and skills, practitioners need to be seriously involved in all aspects of program development and instruction, they need to accept responsibility and ownership for their own learning, and they need to demonstrate rigor and inventiveness in planning and refining. Middle level principals have the same desires. They want to take charge of their own education by regularly enrolling in university courses and training programs to upgrade their skills, they want to engage in intellectual dialogues and debate, and they want to determine their own professional needs and growth.

Given the opportunity to participate in the inservice planning process, recipients feel empowered and more open to learn. True learning must be something principals do, not something others do *to* or *for* them. Principals were clear when describing their preferred learning styles and identifying their different interests and needs:

> When principals go to inservices at the superintendent's level or cluster level, they resist because they see it all coming from the top down. People who create the inservices should identify the areas that need improvement and then discuss these issues with the building level administrators. They can't continue to start from the top down. (19)

Instead of attending mandated seminars, ask the administrators what they need and want, as opposed to the uselessness of the seminars we have to attend. (20)

Rather than the district telling me I have to attend, I need to figure out what I need to attend myself. I would rather participate in study groups and discuss books with other administrators. I need the time and opportunity to read. (21)

2) Reflection within the school context and sharing with other colleagues. A 1985 study of managers showed that they learned 50 percent of their jobs on the job; 20 percent from education and training; and the remaining 30 percent from coworkers, bosses, and mentors (Zembe, 1985). To fully realize that last 30 percent, principals must network with their peers and take advantage of the expertise of their fellow colleagues. Principals regard their cohort experience as primary to their learning. In a recent study of expressed needs of urban middle school principals, Neufeld (1997) found that principals "came to rely on their colleagues as individuals with whom they could share their shortcomings as well as their strengths, as individuals who could assist them and whom they could assist" (p. 504).

Many of the principals interviewed for this study also value the opportunity to be givers as well as receivers of ideas, services, and skills. The process of being helpful, of sharing experiences with colleagues, and of becoming a resource for others is one of the most powerful ways for principals to generate insight into their own work. Their desire to converse frequently, to talk at length about what they do and why they do it, and to discuss areas of leadership, substantiates Evans and Mohr's (1999) point that while principals' learning is personal, it takes place most effectively while working in groups. As middle level principals attempt different approaches, they obviously need the opportunity to discuss adaptations they make and to solve problems they encounter.

It's good to hear that other people have the same problems I do. Colleague interaction is good; you come back feeling refreshed. The camaraderie and spirit of being with people who do the same thing as I do is great. You get a bigger picture of where you are, and it gives you more of a reality basis instead of just relying on yourself. (19)

Provide principals with the opportunity to interact with fellow principals
. . . getting out and walking in each other's shoes offers you a different
perspective. (34)

Seminar kinds of programs where they bring practicing and perspective
administrators together and they have an opportunity to talk and exchange ideas. We need discussion more in the trenches . . . collaboration
with other colleagues . . . hearing those nuances, the way others do something . . . having access to different districts, documents, handbooks, and
things like that. (04)

Networking . . . need support of a critical group of friends, people you
can call . . . share strategies and ideas, dialogue professionally, problem
solve, vent. (32)

In addition to networking with supportive colleagues, many middle
level principals desire instruction on how to become reflective and an-
alytical about their own learning and leadership style. With the school
campus as their focal point, they want to question their practice, think
about why they engage in certain activities, and attempt authentic
change. According to Johnson (1994), we "must confront practitioners
with contentious ideas and conflicting explanations of events. Only
then will they foster independent thinking and promote a true spirit of
inquiry and reflection in the field of school administration" (p. 16).

Many of the practicing middle level principals in our sample desire
to learn more about themselves and want to become reflective practitioners who participate in collaborative activities and collegial strategies. By encouraging different ways of thinking about common problems, by transforming school problems into opportunities for school
improvement, by offering opportunities for shared problem solving and
reflection, and by providing a context of mutual support and trust in
which personal relationships may be established and developed, professional development offerings can be very effective. The principals
acknowledge that even though focused reflection takes them away
from the work, it is essential. After all, "by far the most significant
learning experiences in adulthood involve critical self-reflection—reassessing the way we have posed problems and reassessing our own
orientation to perceiving, knowing, believing, and acting (Mezirow &
Associates, 1990, p. 13).

Reflecting on practice, understanding team building, understanding systems and organizational structures . . . very important, critical for success. (11)

Needs for professional development can be met best by convincing principals that they can take the time to go . . . we need to grow professionally and personally . . . to do this job effectively, we need to truly understand ourselves, our motives, our biases . . . this takes time and reflection. (17)

We need time to be able to read and digest the volumes of work that are coming out, time to be able to sit and discuss with colleagues, time to go to conferences and come back and implement instead of picking up the pieces. (20)

3) Systematic development supported by district time, money, and resources. "One of the paradoxes of professional development is that it can be both energy and time depleting and energy and time replenishing" (Barth, 1986, p. 157). Too often, though, the inservice experience seems to fade surprisingly quickly with little to no real benefit. Districts and professional organizations would be wise to keep this in mind and recognize that it is important for development to be ongoing and to be part of the normal set of routines. Principals need time to read, understand, and reflect on research about instructional issues in order to make sound educational decisions. They need training that is proactive; takes place over a long period of time; and provides opportunities for them to try new skills in their schools, review their impact, discuss them at the next inservice session, and then attempt refinements. Using a systematic approach with specific objectives and intrinsic incentives for participation will help middle level principals learn to take risks, forward the reform efforts, and improve schools for students. Participants expressed strongly the need for a supportive district culture that provides them with opportunities to observe, consult with, and be mentored by the best; to be rewarded for making sustainable changes; and to be encouraged to take risks.

The best knowledge I got was working as an assistant principal under a great mentor. I observed his decision-making, problem-solving, delegation, and monitoring skills. I found that shadowing another principal who really understands the concepts of middle school is invaluable. I suggest pulling the best people and setting up mentoring programs where you can be exposed to a variety of different leadership styles. (19)

Give an administrator time to mentor somebody . . . time to think, time to talk, time to plan, those types of things . . . give an overall view of what administration is like. In terms of sharing, it's good for the mentor to reevaluate what and why they are doing certain things. (29)

It's a time issue with me. It's like how much am I going to devote myself to these inservices? What am I going to get out of it? When I'm there, I'm away from the building so there's a trade-off there. Will the district be supportive? (22)

National organizations can't know what each school district needs . . . that's a local concern that school districts ought to take upon themselves. They should know what the communal personalities happen to be and what they want, like going into the field and observing other administrators. Why stay within our own district? Why not offer incentives? (31)

4) Competent instructors using practical, adult learning processes. Evans and Mohr (1999) stated that "teaching principals how to lead schools by giving them predigested 'in-basket' training hardly leads to new thinking about leadership, teaching, or learning" (p. 531). They believe that "learning experiences for principals must be intellectually rigorous and provoke the questioning of long-held assumptions" (p. 531). In other words, effective professional development is no longer an event done *for* or done *to* administrators. The mode of instruction must be designed to accomplish more than mere transmission of information. Principals must be placed in the role of genuine learner and prodded to rethink their goals, purposes, knowledge, and skills.

Competent trainers actually model problem-solving approaches, get the principals engaged in their own learning, and ask a lot of "why" and "how" questions. Good instructors role-play exercises and then encourage analysis of administrative thinking and reflection based on true-to-life case studies and personal experiences. Different sets of problems are used for self-conscious analysis of administrative responses. Quality professional development programs demand that participants identify and evaluate alternative ways of fulfilling their responsibilities, challenge them to reflect on the effects of value judgements and preconceptions of administrative action, and encourage principals to make adaptations where necessary. Practicing middle level principals don't want to be told what to do. They'd rather be provoked to think about their reasons for their actions and to consider (assess) the impact of those actions. Participants share multiple ways in which trainers can structure activities so that principals can practice components of their new roles, identify strengths and weaknesses, and bridge the glaring gaps in knowledge.

> How to do this, how to do that . . . instead of telling me how to do, I would have liked to experience it myself. Somebody reading a book at me doesn't work. I would like to see a lot more hands-on activities . . . actually opening up my eyes. (26)

> Practical, practical, practical . . . theory builds a base, but the practical skills are equally important. We need interaction with others and more on-the-job experiences . . . exercises need to be connected to the real world; we need opportunities to apply theory. (42)

> Go and observe . . . do it versus talking about it . . . get out, see what others are doing, develop usable rosters and flexible schedules, plan budgets, order supplies, work with a team of teachers in getting parents involved . . . we need actual experience in certain areas to be able to feel competent, and we need quality instructors or trainers to help us . . . those who know how it really is. (21)

Synopsis: How do middle level principals learn best? Under what conditions will middle level principals become committed, sustained, lifelong learners in their important work of forwarding reform? There seems to be some general agreement in several areas. Principals' knowledge, skill, and sense of efficacy can be enhanced by professional development that incorporates and values the following criteria:

- Professional development for middle level principals should be based on their expressed needs and should involve participants in the planning, implementing, and evaluating of such activities.

- Professional development for middle level principals should take place in a supportive cohort structure that promotes reflection on local school needs and sharing among fellow colleagues.
- Professional development for middle level principals should be long-term and backed by time, money, and resources from the district.
- Professional development for middle level principals should be conducted by competent presenters who use adult learning processes in addressing practical issues.

SUMMARY

Barth (1986) believes that if we can devise ways to help principals "reflect thoughtfully and systematically upon the work they do, analyze that work, clarify their thinking through spoken and written articulation, and engage in conversations with others about that work, they will better understand their complex schools, the tasks confronting them, and their own styles as leaders" (p. 160). This exploration of practicing middle level principals and their perceptions of professional development demonstrates agreement.

Most of the interviewees acknowledge that understanding practice is an important precondition for improving practice and that an integral part of improving the effectiveness of the school necessitates that professional development be an ongoing process. However, as Little (1993) reminded us, the process is complicated, takes time, and requires models of good practices and coaching support. It works best in the company of others and in an environment that encourages risk-taking designed to improve student learning.

A visual presentation of the influences upon the professional development of middle level principals would see three fundamental sources interacting to provide the knowledge and skills necessary to administering a middle school. These three are further linked to an environment setting of supplemental—yet critical—influencing factors (*See* figure 5.1).

The prime areas of figure 5.1, including (1) the knowledge base, (2) personal and professional assessment, and (3) the world of practice, become the foundation of sound development for the middle level principal. This paradigm for program building must then be set in an envi-

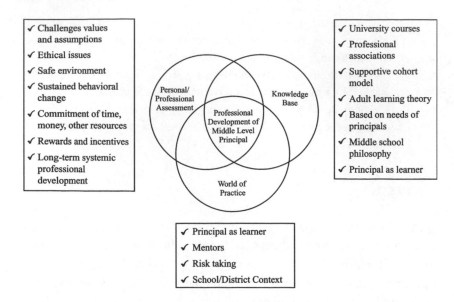

✓ Challenges values and assumptions
✓ Ethical issues
✓ Safe environment
✓ Sustained behavioral change
✓ Commitment of time, money, other resources
✓ Rewards and incentives
✓ Long-term systemic professional development

Personal/ Professional Assessment

Knowledge Base

Professional Development of Middle Level Principal

World of Practice

✓ University courses
✓ Professional associations
✓ Supportive cohort model
✓ Adult learning theory
✓ Based on needs of principals
✓ Middle school philosophy
✓ Principal as learner

✓ Principal as learner
✓ Mentors
✓ Risk taking
✓ School/District Context

Figure 5.1. Influences on the Professional Development of Middle Level Principals

ronment of the multiple affecting agents in the societal and professional world as identified in the figure.

We must continue to discuss and explore the what, where, and how of middle school principals' professional development. Although the voice of the principal is typically absent in the planning or study of professional development, this study focused on that voice and acknowledged that involving principals in their own development is both desired and warranted. Findings also indicate that continuous education of middle school principals can be useful in the rapidly changing, increasingly complex environment of today's middle level schools.

In summary, the format, questions, and challenges of preparing middle level principals continue to seek a focus and answers. The middle school reform agenda will not find all the answers in past practices. A new paradigm must be the goal in educational administration program and preparation models.

Responsiveness to the School and Community

Laying a New Foundation: Exploration, Education, and *Edification* Before *Implementation*

While leadership for the 21st century is defined by Rost (1991) as an influence relationship among leaders and collaborators who intend real changes that reflect mutual purposes, developmentally responsive middle level principals also realize that "wholesale changes in an organization can dramatically affect overall morale, productivity, and turnover" (Deal, 1985, p. 294). Given this fact, chapter 6 outlines the strategies that today's middle school leaders use *before* implementing reform initiatives. If the change process includes three broad phases, then the first, initiation, incorporates the process that leads up to the decision to change. Drawing on the work of Miles (1986) and others, Fullan (1991) argues that initiation depends on three "Rs": (1) relevance of the improvement innovation in terms of need, quality, practicality, clarity, and complexity; (2) readiness of the staff to become involved; and (3) resource and support availability, including time. The principals interviewed for this study refer to these initiation phases as exploration, education, and edification.

According to the interviewees, the process respects honesty and diversity of thought and opinion. It involves an initial exploration of possible change areas, followed by discussions and education regarding the issues involved, and finally built through support, commitment, and ownership. In their own words, the respondents reflect upon the importance of time, communication, openness, and appreciation. Responsive middle school principals share a vision for improvement and growth, work diligently at laying a foundation for change, investigate fully the rationale underpinning reform, and dialogue passionately with purpose. Above all, they are sensitive and appreciate the need for time, training, trust, and tangible support prior to transformation.

EXPLORATION

Theme six outlines the strategies that today's responsive middle level leaders use *before* implementing reform initiatives. Recognizing that "there is always a tremendous responsibility in change . . . a great opportunity to make an enormous difference" (09), developmentally responsive middle level leaders willingly accept their role as catalyst. Even within the context of political pressures and limited resources, as true change agents they understand that the process needs to respect honesty and diversity of thought and opinion. According to Fullan (1999), "schools that manage change best are those with a collaborative work culture" (p. 1). The interviewees agree. "You need to be able to work well with people . . . to accept different ideas. It's very important to do things collaboratively" (03). It involves an initial exploration of possible change areas, a "thorough examination of all the components that make a good middle school" (04), "careful preparation" (10), and sound rationale. Teachers need "time to just sit and talk . . . to kick around their ideas . . . become a group of people working toward the same end" (06).

Courage to Change

"No single individual is more important to initiating and sustaining improvement in middle grades school students' performance than the school principal" (Jackson & Davis, 2000, p. 157). Given this fact, developmentally responsive leaders need courage to take on the role of principal change agent, to set the intellectual and interpersonal tone of the school, and to shape the organizational conditions under which the school community works (Hipp, 1997). "No change is easy and most change is met with some resistance" (20). Even so, effective schools continually evaluate themselves and make improvements. Evaluation begins by involving stakeholders in planning, establishing goals, and specifying measurable outcomes. One practicing middle school principal said it involves, "Constantly doing a needs assessment, a personal needs assessment of what's wrong. Then setting a goal, prioritizing the goal and coming up with a plan to achieve the goal. Implement the plan involving staff, resources, timeline, etc. Evaluate and ask if the need still exists" (19). In their own words, other respondents reflect upon the importance of time, communication, openness, and appreciation.

Have to see the world as it is, have the ability to deal with change and utilize the tools that will help you deal with it, understand the diverse cultures and have the courage to deal with problems. When you change a school, you change its culture. (19)

Most people are afraid of change but you can really learn from it. I think that our school has learned a lot from the changes we made and I'm proud of that. I complement people on new ideas and am willing to implement them where necessary. (26)

There's a real human side to change, too. You have to be really respectful of the culture and the traditions. So, it's a balance of all that. I think the key to change is understanding the culture and working to create the culture that you want. (11)

Plan to Involve

Research has demonstrated that schools that have restructured to function democratically "produce high achievement with more students of all abilities and graduate more of them with better levels of skills and understanding than traditional schools do" (Darling-Hammond, 1997, p. 331). Studies also show that "student achievement increases substantially in schools with collaborative [democratic] work cultures that foster a professional learning community among teachers and others, focus continually on improving instructional practices in light of student performance data, and link to standards and staff development" (Fullan, 1998, p. 8). In other words, it appears that "when given support, time, and resources, democracy of, by, and with 'workers' works" (Glickman, 1998, p. 80).

Shared decision making, a process of making educational decisions in a collaborative manner at the school level, emphasizes the fact that those closest to the children will make the best decisions about children's education. It hinges on the belief that those carrying out decisions should have a voice in determining the decisions. The purpose, according to Bauer (1992) and Lange (1993), is to improve school effectiveness and student learning by increasing staff commitment and ensuring that schools are more responsive to the needs of students. Intensive, lasting change will not occur if the school community is opposed, or even if it is indifferent (Balfanz & Mac Iver, 1998). Newmann (1991) suggests that giving teachers more autonomy, discretion, and control in conducting their work will encourage a greater sense of ownership of, and responsibility for, quality in student learning. While the analysis of the data collected for this study supports these findings, it also highlights the necessity for sensitivity, awareness and administrative balance in overseeing the shared decision-making process.

At an early stage of development, we are reminded by Stevenson and Erb (1998) that "teacher quality of life influences school climate. Yet as school climate improves, the teacher quality of life gets even better. Positive changes build on each other—creating a mutually supportive momentum for continuing progress" (p. 52). Administrators and teachers alike need to work together in finding that mutually supportive balance, especially with regard to decision-making power. "Wise principals realize that as much as possible, those closest to the teaching/learning situation need to make important judgments pertaining to it and affecting their students and themselves" (Arnold & Stevenson, 1998, p. 40).

However, striking that balance is easier said than done. Exemplary middle schools and their leaders find it essential to involve all stakeholders in the change process. They work diligently at mobilizing a critical mass of school staff members, parents, and others to 'buy in' to the proposed changes. According to Hatch and Hytten (1997), "involving the public in setting district goals and plans may result in more agreement on education goals than is currently evident, as well as more community ownership of planned reforms" (p. 6). Successful school reform involves a shift from controlling and directing at the top level to guiding and facilitating at all the levels. When conducted collaboratively, the change process can contribute to a school culture that demonstrates cooperation, meaningful involvement, and dedication to continuous improvement. *Turning Points* (Carnegie Council on Adolescent Development, 1989) calls for empowering teachers to make such decisions and to share the responsibility for school leadership. Developmentally responsive middle level leaders understand that those who know and work with students daily must be trusted to do what is best for them.

> Absolutely, inviting as many people as possible into the decision-making processes. I feel that all of the stakeholders, whether it be the parents, students, teachers, or staff, have to be involved. They need to have at least an opportunity to contribute in some way. Always be aware of what is happening and why it's happening and how it's going to affect them. I think when they feel part of that then they feel more comfortable with the decisions that are made. (29)

> You need to have done your homework to know what part of the change you want. You have to know your building and the community to know whether or not they'll accept the change, and you have to get people involved in helping you bring about the change. Get people involved and give responsibility. (20)

> A very cohesive staff; a staff who knows how to collaborate and make decisions without the principal having to say "do this" or "do that." I have spent a lot of time training the teachers on how to solve problems together. (21)

"Attempts to 'package' reform initiatives through the programmatic efforts of nationally recognized educators often ignore the spirit of the local; as a result, they may simply impose more demands on teachers and pupils alike, and thereby contribute to their alienation from community" (Foster, cited in Merz & Furman, 1997, p. ix). If the administration exercises too much authority, whether in the interest of time efficiency or out of a need to be in control, group members will have less investment in real change. Unless all of the stakeholders are involved early and often in the initial stages of visioning and planning, implementing reform will become just another authoritarian mandate met with resistance and lack of support. Indeed, instead of positive outcomes being realized, negative consequences can actually flourish. If the mode of operation of an organization is too hierarchical, manipulating, or threatening, group members may become overly dependent on the structures and unable to operate without directives. Administrators who are reluctant to loosen the reins and allow teachers to assume more control over the process necessary to remake the educational enterprise will be unsuccessful in their efforts to implement change. It is important to remember that responsibility comes with practice and empowerment.

Be Open to Explore

In addition to courage and the foresight to involve all stakeholders, true reform requires a desire to delve deeply and an openness to explore thoroughly. As Fullan and Miles (1992) explain, "change goes best when it is carried out by a cross-role group. . . . In such a group, different worlds collide, more learning occurs, and change is realistically managed" (p. 247). One participant's way of ensuring that all relevant groups understand the work underway and their part in making it successful is called the 'huddle.' "Every Tuesday my staff and I come together and we share the agenda making and facilitating. What's the game plan for the week? What's going well and what hasn't? We discuss problems, where we've been, where we're going, and plans to get there" (18).

An educator must be a "reflective practitioner" who considers carefully how actions are implemented and what the resulting effects are (Fullan & Hargreaves, 1996, p. 67). Educators must accept moral responsibility for educating young adolescent middle level students, have sufficient autonomy and resources to encourage educational entrepreneurship in the development of new programs, and possess a deep-seeded commitment to such reform efforts in their schools. When they work together to govern the school and make critical decisions about curriculum and school policy, a climate of innovation and experimentation is common, and a feeling of empowerment and growth is nurtured. "A cooperative learning community means a more comfortable and inspiring work environment for teachers as well as students" (Graves, 1992, p. 62).

It's important to be open to trying things in a different way . . . changing the plan if it's not working and being able to take a risk . . . willingness to make accommodations and adaptations, to get out of the box . . . looking at a problem from more than one point of view. (06)

Needs assessment so that you're building change around some kind of perceived needs and data. I think change should always be goal-oriented, and it should involve the stakeholders. It should be slow and steady progress that lasts longer than knee-jerk reactions. You need to hear the voices of many. (33)

If you're very clear, you're very directed, you don't rush into it, and you let the process flow, that helps people to not resist. Look at all the pros and cons of the program, visit, read the literature, go to your staff as much as possible, and know deep down in your heart that it's the best thing for the kids. (13)

EDUCATION

Discussions and education regarding the issues involved need to follow and expand upon the initial exploration stage. Developmentally responsive middle level principals share a vision for continuous improvement and growth, work diligently at laying a foundation for change, investigate fully the rationale underpinning reform, and dialogue passionately with purpose. Their role is to help various stakeholders develop sufficient knowledge about both the need for a schoolwide improvement process and the nature of the proposed changes so that their constituencies can make informed decisions. While discussing the difficulty of change, one principal shared the importance of "taking on the philosophy before the practicality of doing it" (07), so as to avoid future "battles." Another principal advised the following, "Clarifying the objective at the outset minimizes the teachers' anxiety and resistance" (10).

According to Cuban (1983), transforming typically large, uncompromising school bureaucracies into communities characterized by a context of difference and a commitment of collaboration requires change beyond mere surface restructuring. Such transformation neces-

sitates identifying structural and institutional arrangements vital to promoting ongoing staff development (Darling-Hammond & McLaughlin,
1995) and introducing processes that change existing professional values and norms in ways that support the creation of school-wide professional communities (Fullan, 1995). Argyris and Schon (1978) believe
that these transformative actions require schools to examine basic
premises that guide organizational behavior and to continuously increase the existing organizational knowledge base. Murphy (1991)
adds, "Real educational transformation will require the involvement of
all key players, work on all components of the system, and the simul-
taneous use of four distinct but interrelated restructuring strategies—
teacher empowerment, school-based management, choice, and teaching for understanding. Reminded that effective reform initiatives
involve a "willingness to put in the time, effort and energy in terms of
planning" (04), listen to the following advice:

> You need to give people exposure to information, present them with
> ideas, and make them part of the ownership. It comes back to collabora-
> tion. We bring people in, teacher to teacher, to describe, explain, clarify.
> It's all about educating before implementing. (24)

> If you're going to live in the real world, you need to have a central office
> and a school board that's going to make a commitment to the staff de-
> velopment necessary to make these programs work. To make this con-
> cept work, it all goes back to selling the teachers on why you are doing
> it and then providing the training necessary to do it. (04)

> If you're going to change the way something is organized, put as much
> of it out there and up front as you can. Then communicate, communicate,
> communicate. This way everybody knows what is involved in the
> change, and there are no surprises. (06)

> We try to figure out what to do and how to do it. We go to conferences
> here, there, and everywhere. We get people cranked up, encourage them
> to take risks. We do this, try that . . . we allow teachers in the decision-
> making process as much as possible. (11)

EDIFICATION

As evidenced throughout the middle school movement, organizational change alone will not alter dramatically the educational experiences of middle grade students. "Developmental responsiveness carries with it major implications for school restructuring. It demands that middle level educators move beyond the "mere" form of middle level programs, such as interdisciplinary teaming and teacher advisories, and become increasingly concerned with the substance of these programs" (Lounsbury & Clark, 1990, p. 134). Mergendoller (1993) argues that many middle schools have made the recommended structural changes and that they often represent "cosmetic fiddling" (p. 444), failing to result in fundamental changes in the purposes, priorities, and functioning of the school. Authentic change is considerably more complex than simply implementing a promising idea for a term or a year and then comparing changes in student achievement or performance in specific areas. Attempting to bring about more positive student outcomes by selecting one or two of the Carnegie recommendations is not nearly as powerful a strategy for change as attempting to implement most or all of the elements. They were envisioned to be interactive. In fact, according to Stevenson and Erb (1998), "manipulation of one or even a few variables is insufficient to bring about the more expansive re-direction of schooling that *Turning Points* calls for" (p. 50).

Researchers, practitioners, and policymakers have come together in the movement to reform middle level schools; but the most difficult task—implementing those reforms—must be in the hands of practitioners who are informed about the important issues in middle level education and about young adolescent development. They are more likely to make the kind of changes in their schools that will have a major effect on school restructuring (Clark & Clark, 1994).

> Invite people into the change. I can't change it; we have to do this collectively. We have to ask what makes sense for Tommy . . . bringing them back to purpose . . . lots of dialogue with lots of people . . . building trust, being consistent, working hard, building respect. (09)

Well, any changes that I need to have happen or take place among the staff necessitate them buying into the change first. So I have to find a way every time, depending on what it is, to let the staff buy into it. Sometimes it can be informal conversations with the folks that you know are the leaders. They come up with the ideas themselves and run with that thought. Sometimes you have to talk to your most negative people first and get that out of the way. It depends on what the issue is or what the change is, but universally speaking the staff has to buy into it before any change can exist. You might as well be talking to the brick wall if you don't have the staff buy into it. (32)

Provide Support

Middle level reform—indeed all school reform—is a developmental process. According to Stevenson and Erb (1998), "it begins by teachers believing in and wanting to change" (p. 52). Exploration is accompanied by education and edification, i.e., creating opportunities for change and learning the skills necessary to support it. With a supportive environment and changes in practice, reforms get established. The authors remind us that "as the reforms are established, they change the way a school works and the way teachers and students experience school. Then, and only then can we expect to see real improvement in student performance and behavior" (p. 52).

Without exception, the respondents of this study were future-oriented and expressed hopes, dreams, and goals for the future of their school. They recognized that change sometimes must be incremental, and they expressed patience and a willingness to let important changes come about over time. Above all, developmentally responsive middle level leaders are sensitive and appreciate the need for time, training, trust, and tangible support prior to transformation. "We need time to interact around progress. Teachers need time to reflect. It's a rare individual that will make the transfer without those things" (08). Built through honesty, awareness, support, commitment, and ownership, the process of edification is vital. It involves "bringing significant parties together, making them part of the planning, helping them to be educated with you, building leadership in everyone, and realizing that we're all partners here" (32). According to Anderman and Urdan

(1995), "meaningful leadership is possible only when supported by leadership at the classroom, school, district and state levels" (p. 26). The principals here believe that "If you want a successful school, you can't do it yourself. Look at the strength of your staff, delegate to people, provide support, accept mistakes, and go on" (44). Others agree:

> You've got to make sure that the teachers are absolutely buying into it. They require coaching. The administration really has to be keyed into it. They require a tremendous amount of support. And so, you need to work very hard. (07)

> Our school board has been very, very supportive in terms of personnel dollars. They have appropriated funds to go into programs and initiatives that we have decided are important. (23)

> My approach with teachers is that I respect their talents and that any success we experience in this school will be directly attributed to their co-operation and talents. I always ask people to be willing to try new ideas, and I give them the confidence that they are not going to be penalized if it doesn't work. The goal is always to improve things for students, and if their intentions and my intentions are the same then there is little that we can't accomplish. (34)

Build Trust and Consensus

Providing a caring, trusting work environment and ample opportunity for participation and shared decision making are two of the ways that organizations enlist people's commitment and involvement at all levels (Bolman & Deal, 1993). According to one of the principals, "Moral and ethical leadership allows teachers, parents and kids to trust in the school. They always know there is honesty, integrity, mutual respect, and trust that creates a culture in a school that allows all things to be possible. The culture is characterized by trust and the belief that teachers are respected and have the power to make their own decisions" (33). Even skeptical and unsure teachers will be won over when they realize their views are heard and valued and when they see that they have the power to shape school policies based on what they know and discover to be best for the students (Kilgore, Webb, & the Faculty of

Coral Springs Middle School, 1997). Succinctly stated by one interviewee, "The first piece of this is analysis, the second is dialogue and the
third is consensus building. What emerges, you hope, is a certain level
of consensus on a vision, on what's doable and what isn't. People become more comfortable in the decision-making process" (22).

Substantial change requires time and continuity to be more self-
aware through reflection, processing, and debriefing. Interactions between people that consist of sustained transactions and that are developed around common goals, joint tasks, important sharings, and
meeting one another's needs on a daily, weekly, or regular basis are all
necessary when trying to develop ties of community and the skills
needed to work together well. Only when people regularly meet, work,
and play together does a deeper connection arise. Time to meet and
time to mesh must be adequately provided and sacredly guarded.
Change is an evolutionary processes that just take time—a fact, warn
Arnold and Stevenson (1998), that building administrators need to remember in their hurried world of do-it-now directives from the district
office. In the absence of such factors, reform cannot be created, mandated, or even declared into existence. Evidenced by the participants'
comments, imposing conformity tends to breed resistance.

> All changes have to be agreed upon by the teachers to the extent possi-
> ble. Form committees, put ideas on paper, get staff to agree on it—con-
> sensus building model. (21)

> Change requires a conversation. Typically I go to the stakeholders and
> invite them into a conversation because change is an evolution, not a rev-
> olution. You need to be sensitive and invite those who are going to be
> part of the change, whether it's going to affect them or they're going to
> be responsible for implementing it. So I seek the thinking of others and
> balance it with what I am attempting to try. (25)

> Many administrators go to outside people to fix their problems. I don't
> do that. My faculty has trust in what I bring to them. They resist some
> things but we discuss things and they tend to trust. They have an open fo-
> rum, there is a give and take regarding change. (31)

First thing you have to do is establish a relationship of trust with the people. Get their input into the change, what are the effects, and what they think; if you can, try to pilot it, then evaluate, and then implement. (35)

SUMMARY

"Given the enormity and complexity of their mission, it is increasingly clear that if middle schools, indeed all schools, are to be successful in educating children for the future, then they need the assistance of an active and engaged community" (Sanders, 2001, p. 53). Developmentally responsive middle level leaders couldn't agree more. "There are these people called stakeholders. All of us are stakeholders. The kids are stakeholders, the parents are stakeholders, the secretaries are stakeholders, the teachers are stakeholders, I am a stakeholder. The community is a stakeholder, and I think it's important to see how all the stakeholders view the culture" (27). This statement from a respondent, along with the numerous quotes stated above, underlines the importance of, and value in, working well with students, parents, and community members in exchanging ideas and resources and fostering collegial relationships that enhance the environment. Developmentally responsive middle level schools are characterized by such family and community partnerships (NMSA, 1995). According to one respondent, they require

Resourcefulness; vision; know how to reach out and create collaborative partnerships with businesses, communities, families, and universities; to find other funding; teach teachers the value of grant writing; to be a teacher of teachers; to demonstrate daily the ability to interact with teachers and children; to bring people together within a building by listening to others; to find resources beyond the building; and to reach out to other middle schools. (18)

"School competence results from the interaction between children, their various environments, and their families' and communities' previous experience, rather than from a single factor, such as the school, the home, or the child's natural environments" (Bowman, 1994, p. 69). Section III of this book highlights Comer's (1988) basic premise that "a working partnership among the school staff, the students, and their families . . . [can result] in an emotional bond" (p. 50) between these groups and in shared commitment to work toward the well-being of the school and its students. Although it involves an acceptance of different ideas and an acknowledgement of different, and often conflicting, needs, everyone involved benefits. According to one third-year principal, it's a bit of a juggling act. "You juggle a lot of balls when you're an administrator. You're trying to satisfy four or five different publics, and you have to learn the balances" (15). In addition to being a balancing act, it is also a role-modeling act. "When students see several adults cooperating, speaking civilly, sharing responsibilities, and supporting each other during the years, they are viewing powerful illustrations of how to be successful adults" (Burkhardt, 1997, p. 174).

Developmentally responsive middle level leaders take their positions and their responsibilities very seriously. We are reminded by Valentine, Maher, Quinne, and Irvin (1999) that the 1996 Interstate School Leaders Licensure Consortium (ISLLC) outlines four common standards of school leadership. The fourth standard reads: "A school administrator is an educational leader who promotes the success of all students by collaborating with families and community members, responding to diverse community interests and needs, and mobilizing community resources" (p. 55). Indeed, this is an image for which middle level leaders participating in this study gave numerous illustrations. This chapter and the next are replete with practical, persuasive, and effective ways to link schooling with the surrounding community. Such events intersect personal and social concerns and address young adolescents' need for meaningful participation in school and community happenings.

Flexibility Is the Name of the Game: Ambiguity and Chaos Are Not the Same!

"Flexibility is often portrayed positively as a necessary characteristic of highly effective people. Principals who can adapt to change, who are able to bend without breaking, and who are resilient in the face of adversity are great role models for today's versatile students" (Brown, 1999, p. 147). Chapter 7 recalls the attributes mentioned in the previous chapters and promotes flexibility as the umbrella trait for developmentally responsive middle level principals. The "nature of the beast," the ever-changing undulating temperament of early adolescents, requires a tolerance for chaos. Responsive principals go a step beyond tolerance and actually admit that they are energized by the unpredictableness of middle school students. They have an innate openness to noise, mess, diversity, challenges, and changes. They tout flexibility as the key in scheduling, role defining, community involving, relating, and problem solving.

ENERGIZED BY THE UNPREDICTABLENESS

The seventh theme recalls the attributes mentioned in the previous six responses and promotes flexibility as the umbrella trait for developmentally responsive middle level leadership. The "nature of the beast" (14) so to speak, the ever changing, "undulating temperament of early adolescents" (09), requires a "tolerance for chaos" (07). A "level of calmness" (08), "an ability to react to many situations at one time" (13), and a knack for dealing with ambiguity and uncertainty, are all characteristics of effective, responsive leadership (Neufeld, 1997).

In fact, effective middle level educators "must have a 'tolerance for turbulence' and be able to enjoy rather than be upset by, the mercurial behavior of these young people" (Arth, Lounsbury, McEwin, & Swaim, 1995). Lounsbury and Vars (1978) warn against misinterpreting what could appear to be a homogeneity among young adolescents; thinking that all 10–14 year olds are the same. They tell us that it is not so much that these young adolescents are alike, rather, "their lack of similarity is what they have in common" (p. 25). Research by Wiles and Bondi (1981, p. 30) represented in table 7.1 depicts the extreme differences in the rate and scale of growth and development among young adolescents.

Table 7.1 Portrait of a 13-Year-Old

6 feet 2 inches in height	or	4 feet 7 inches
So awkward that she trips going up the stairs	or	Olympic gold medal winner with a perfect 10.0 in parallel bar competition
Alcoholic, drug addict	or	Sunday school leader, Little leaguer
Wears mouth braces	or	Competes in Miss Teenage America
Turned off and looking forward to quitting school	or	Curious and enthusiastic learner
Unable to read the comic page	or	Reads the *Wall Street Journal*
Has trouble with whole numbers	or	Can solve geometry problems
A regular in juvenile court	or	An Eagle Scout
Already a mother of two	or	Still plays with dolls

George and Alexander (1993) concur by reminding us that "middle school students seem to have little in common with each other developmentally, except that they have so little in common" (p. 301). Even the principals interviewed here state that "There's a predictability in their unpredictability . . . the constant change, the energy level . . . it's an exciting, challenging time" (08). Manning (1993) adds to the discussion by highlighting the "rapid, dramatic" changes that occur in the 10- to 14-year-old students. "Physical changes can be seen almost daily" (p. 35). Developmentally responsive leaders are aware of the potpourri of adolescent behaviors, growth spurts, mood swings, strong opinions, and preoccupation with self that vacillates from tears to laughter, high energy to fatigue, excitable to lethargic behavior. Recognizing that "very few developmental periods are characterized by as many changes in as many areas" (Eccles & Wigfield, 1997, p. 15), responsive principals practice patient and persistence in relating to their students' individuality. Listen to their innate openness to noise, mess, diversity, and challenges:

> I try to be patient and understand and recognize the changes they will be going through. There's a lot of "posturing" going on. They really need a social setting where they can be safe, comfortable, make mistakes, and learn from them. "Flexible" is the key word for the middle school principal. (16)

> When I'm walking down the hallway I'm looking inside some classrooms to see what's going on. I want to see desks clustered. I want to see messes. I want to hear noise. I want to see hands-on learning. I want to see different things happening. I want us to learn the way young adolescents learn. I want us to be very aware of the needs of the kids and give them the support necessary. (14)

> I think anything that you do that deals with developmental aspects is real important. . . . [For example] instructional activities that are active in nature, cooperative learning, literature circles, all those things that give kids an opportunity to interact, recognizing that middle level kids are highly social in nature. It's exciting. (22)

Literature on leadership suggests that effective middle level principals exhibit a high tolerance for ambiguity and uncertainty when working to effect change, addressing conflicting needs, and responding to conflicting priorities (Goodman & Associates, 1986; Neufeld, 1997; Wheatley, 1992). Almost without exception the middle level principals interviewed for this study support this finding and go a step beyond tolerance and actually admit that they are energized by the unpredictableness of middle school education. They have learned to expect the unexpected and tactfully handle the inexplicable. Erb and Stevenson (1999) note that in fostering growth-inducing environments for students' success, an "energy loop" is created between teachers and students whereby they "invest in students and become in turn energized by their students' responses" (p. 65). As seen in the comments below, this is true for administrators as well.

> Thriving on the energy, not fighting who and what children are. They bring a lot of energy and excitement that I think is stimulating. Accept their curiosity, energy, and a little bit of craziness at times. Work with them and participate in their energy . . . try not to stifle it but to channel it in a way that they maximize what it is they bring. Help them in their social, emotional, and academic development at this particular time as there is much going on. (25)

> The concepts of action are excellent. Thriving on the chaos and the energy. Being a cheerleader and a nurturer of champions. (27)

> The energy level is just so high. The pupils still have respect. They have good days and bad days as far as kids go, but it keeps me young. Because their hormones are raging and they are dealing with a variety of emotions, kids at this age need to talk, work together, and do collaborative types of exercises. (29)

Awareness of young adolescent developmental needs, along with "respect, energy, and a keen excitement for what you are doing" (35), lead developmentally responsive middle level leaders to adopt a very "spontaneous way of doing things because the nature of the youngster is to be spontaneous" (23). In essence, "flexibility comes with the territory" (32). Others agree:

> I'm tough when I need to be and easy when I need to be. I'm very flexible. You have to be flexible in middle level or you will burn out quickly. (21)

> Passion about kids, expertise in their subject or content areas, enthusiasm, contagious enthusiasm, a real desire to connect with kids, and an ability to be flexible. At the middle level you need that delicate balance or skill to harness their energy and enthusiasm and stir it in a positive direction. (24)

TAKING RISKS

In a positive school climate, students, teachers, and administrators alike take risks that foster critical thinking and problem-solving skills. Middle school students respond to a nurturing, safe environment in which they are free to explore and be creative. In order to succeed with this age group, developmentally responsive middle level leaders must be willing to try things, risk failures, learn from their mistakes, and try again. In their study of shared governance and teacher empowerment, researchers Blase and Blase (1994) observed that principals helped teachers improve their instruction and thus improve student achievement. They did this by "permitting and actively encouraging teachers to go beyond the standard or official curriculum—and to do so without the risks and anxieties that typically accompany innovation and occasional failure" (pp. 75–76). When given such autonomy to establish goals, define policies (compatible to systemwide mandates), and organize teaching time and grouping procedures, middle school teams can become schedule and structural risk-takers. Jones (1997) reveals that teams that are allowed to be both creative and spontaneous often feel free to do so. Her findings resulted in teams that were "thoughtful in their planning, interactive in their discussions, rigorous in their academic expectations, and clear in their communications" (p. 215). Developmentally responsive middle level leaders support such autonomy:

> I personally try to empower teachers with the whole notion of accountability and that they are the ones that control how things are accomplished. Communication has to be ongoing and I pride myself as being fully accessible to teachers. I am visible in the school and make sure I am available and that they know what my intentions are. I walk the walk with them so that if there are issues, I am no stranger to them. (34)

> I let my staff be risk-takers and I never say no. My feeling is to try and if it works, share it. I think I have allowed risk-takers to operate that way. It's not that I don't have control of what's going on, but I never want a teacher to feel that they can't try something. I say be a risk-taker and hopefully it will work for the betterment of the youngsters. (23)

What you're all about as a principal is unleashing people, getting people on fire so to speak. If you can create the climate where teachers are coming and saying that I want to try this and I think I can do that, that's what it's all about. (24)

Veteran principals talked about comfort with uncertainty as a strategy for bringing about change. Other self-described risk-takers try to encourage teachers to take the power that is offered to them and work to provide a role model by taking chances with their supervisors. "I try to show teachers that I am willing to hang myself out there and make a commitment to things that have to get done" (07). They believe that this helps teachers become more willing to take chances and build a risk-taking mentality. Several principals mentioned that in order to encourage teachers to engage in decision making, administrators must model such behaviors as well as be willing to live with the results of their deliberations.

You listen; you meet as a group, and then you make a decision and you take a risk as the principal. You implement; and if it doesn't work, you have to take it back and be willing to stand by your mistake and make the necessary changes. (02)

Knowledgeable risk-takers should be able to mediate and negotiate with all their constituents all of the time. Know when to stroke and when to put the hammer down, be flexible, be able to juggle three or four balls at the same time, be organized, a people-person, and a good communicator. (20)

I think people should be risk-takers. We need to be trained to take risks and need to know that we won't get torn apart for taking them. We need to take risks and have a passion and a vision for excellence. (27)

HAVING FUN

There is a certain enthusiasm that accompanies young adolescents. Almost in confessional format, Lockhart (1997) admits that unlike his high school students, his new middle school students "came to class almost exploding with energy; they were spontaneous and funny and surprisingly eager to learn" (pp. 106–107). Developmentally responsive middle level leaders realize that their students have a need for fun and adventure, for new experiences, both educational and recreational. They use humor as an effective social tool to build bridges with students and relieve stress. They model the use of humor as a way of putting their students at ease, as an attention-getter, and as a way to show students that they too are human. Used appropriately, humor can help reduce the psychological distance between people and foster deeper social ties. They also understand that kids at this age are developing a sense of humor on their own and they experiment with what they think is funny. Developmentally responsive middle level principals are open to the humor of kids. In fact, they describe laughter and fun as important factors in both relaxing and enhancing the learning process.

> If I had my pick right now of all of them [schools], I'd stay right where I am. I think the learner, the client, is really a lot of fun to be around. More fun than elementary and high school. The middle school kids are alive, they talk to you, they haven't gone underground yet. It's really a fun place to be. I think it's a neat place, I really do. (30)

> For me it was understanding the importance of visibility. You need to get down and have fun in the classroom with the kids. (32)

There is no doubt that a sense of humor in life goes a long way. Research even demonstrates a positive correlation between laughter and good health, finding that humor is a valuable way to help handle anxiety, anger, and frustration. In this day and age when administrators have to deal with standards, testing, school violence, unrealistic expectations, and waning public support, the need for humor is greater than ever. Faced with the choice to laugh or scream, one participant stated, "I think you have to have a certain wit, you have to laugh a lot because if you don't, you'll go bonkers" (23). The same principal also advocates for "a wild imagination and a high degree of flexibility." For developmentally responsive leaders, the ability to have fun and laugh is paramount. They reveal that those earmarks of the middle school philosophy currently used in their schools (i.e., teaming, exploratories, advisories, looping) have helped to create safe, secure, fun places. Within such an environment, teachers are effective and students learn. In fact, Arth et al. (1995) found that "Conviction, enthusiasm, and a sense of humor were noted as essential qualities for successfully teaching young adolescents" (p. 24). Many expressed their belief that a healthy sense of humor was a necessary ingredient in successful middle level leadership. Being playful, using exaggeration, and telling stories and amusing anecdotes all contribute to having a good time and, as a consequence, learning more. "It shouldn't seem like work. It should be fun. Enjoy what you are doing—just feel it—body language, words, actions, everything!" (17). Others concur:

> We work hard; we play hard. We hold our students to very high standards. I think that you have to have that firmness as a leader; but at the same time, I'm out there in roller blades and I'm part of the club program. I think it's important to model that for your teachers and show your passion. (24)

> There are days when I can get a little crazy because the students are . . . we sure do have a lot more fun. (32)

> Middle school principals need to have lots of energy, be visible, and treat the faculty like you want the students treated. Principals have to be out there, constantly evaluating and planning fun things. It's not all work here; there's plenty of fun too. (35)

> Be willing to do some things that are out of character. For example, you may have to wear a costume or play in a tournament game. (39)

BEING FLEXIBLE AND SPONTANEOUS

George and Alexander (1993) outline characteristics of effective instruction in the middle school explaining that instructional strategies are a combination of structure, balance, and flexibility. Flexibility, according to these researchers, is essential. It is meant "to permit teachers to know when a particular instructional strategy is appropriate and when it is not and the disposition to make the changes in style when it is necessary for the students' benefit to do so" (p. 143). Thus, the nature of the middle school requires adaptability in many areas. Middle school educators must be prepared to make use of intense periods of interest characteristic of the young adolescent. The participants in this study had a high degree of agreement when describing flexibility as a quality of a developmentally responsive middle level principal in the 21st century. "I think they have to be flexible. Flexibility is the name of the game. . . . It takes trying something different every day. . . .. Anything can happen, any day, that makes you have to throw those plans to the wind and try something different" (09).

The informants tout this "flexibility as the name of the game" (09) as the key in scheduling, role defining, community involving, relating, and problem solving. In addition to enjoying their own flexibility in terms of "staffing, teaming, and programming," developmentally responsive middle level leaders are open, willing, and able to give their faculty and staff similar freedom. They "give great latitudes to people that come with great ideas" (04) and encourage them to "manipulate the time for speakers, projects, and group work" (06). They believe that "you've got to be willing to be flexible in the way you do things, how you do things, and when you do things in order to ensure that you give kids their opportunity for success" (07). Other responsive leaders concur:

> I think there's a degree of flexibility that's needed . . . what you're now looking at is a situation where there are so many variables and so many people . . . you need to have the ability to balance. (10)

> The ability to be very flexible and to have spontaneity in the school is a wonderful thing. (02)

Scheduling

Flexible block scheduling, along with interdisciplinary teaming, is included among the six essential program concepts of a middle level school (Alexander & George, 1981). McKay (1995) reports that the daily schedule should feature blocks of instructional time during which interdisciplinary teams of teachers provide appropriate learning experiences for their students. An important characteristic of block scheduling is the development of a schedule within the block of time that can be altered to provide for the regrouping of students.

Flexible and modular scheduling within team teaching structures permits maximum planning and implementation by all team members (Fugate, 1970). With this type of scheduling, teachers on a team are not locked into a fixed number of periods per day or a fixed amount of time per period. For example, an interdisciplinary team of teachers might have a four- or five-period block of time devoted to the academic subject areas. Teachers on the team plan together to determine how they might best use that block of time. The Carnegie Council on Adolescent Development (1989) reports that a key feature of the transformed middle grade school should be flexibility in the duration of classes. "Teacher teams should be able to change class schedules whenever, in their collective professional development, the need exists. They should be able to create blocks of time for instruction that best meet the needs and interests of the students, respond to curriculum priorities, and capitalize on learning opportunities" (p. 52). The 1992 NMSA position paper held that "various organizational arrangements should be utilized with the middle school. . . . No one arrangement is 'best' or 'right' and a middle school should employ varied organizational arrangements" (pp. 16–17). The participants concurred and explained that flexibility extends to a variety of areas:

> You have to be flexible; you [as principal] nccd to have a schedule that provides an opportunity for the teachers to be flexible and do what they feel needs to be done at the time . . . like a juggler; you have to juggle your activities and provide a nice balanced program for your youngsters. (14)

> The bell schedule was here but not quite as flexible as it is now. Teachers who have worked here for more than 10 years are resistant to the flexible block schedule. (19)

> We have flexible scheduling. We have eight periods per day, 45 minutes in length, but because the kids are with a single team, that team can flex that schedule anytime they want. They can have 45 minutes for English one day and then 150 minutes the next. (23)

The primary purpose of using flexible block scheduling for adolescent learners is to support a range of integrated activities. The concept is rooted in concerns about creating sufficient time to immerse students in the learning experience. According to the latest Research Summary supported by NMSA (2000):

> Effective middle level schedules are based on a stated philosophy and goals that must be flexible and responsive to student needs. A flexible and responsive schedule supports blocks of instructional time, appropriate planning time for staff members, advisory time, flexibility for special schedules, and both elective and core programs. The interdisciplinary schedule provides middle school faculties with the freedom and flexibility to design an instructional program that is most responsive to the needs of the young adolescent. The research evidence is clear that a flexible block schedule to support integrated team teaching is the most beneficial to high-quality adolescent learning. (p. 6)

Staffing

The debate over middle level educational reform has often been polarized between the proponents of the intellectual virtues (the cognitive domain) and the advocates of the emotional virtues (the affective domain). Palmer (1993) highlights the fruitlessness of this debate, stating: "The practice of intellectual rigor in the classroom requires an ethos of trust and acceptance. Intellectual rigor depends on things like honest dissent and the willingness to change our minds, things that will not happen if the 'soft' values of community are lacking" (p. xvii). "Balanced teacher and student populations, so that each team is a microcosm of the school at large, are crucial: teachers balanced according to complementing strengths, personal styles, instructional expertise and experience, as well as race, sex and age; students balanced according to sex, achievement, race, exceptionalities and age" (George & Alexander, 1993, p. 290).

The paucity of teachers professionally prepared specifically for middle school is compounded by the reality that middle school teacher preparation programs and advanced degree programs in educational leadership are few (NMSA, 1997). Although there is apparent agreement as to the need for content-strengthened preparation programs for middle school teachers, principals still appear quite divided as to the desirability of secondary- and content-prepared candidates in contrast to those prepared as elementary teachers. When administrators are fortunate enough to have involvement at the initial stages of assembling and staffing a quality middle school, it is important to identify their focus beyond the generalized agreement of content strength within the preparation of the candidate. Personal qualities take a prominent role when principals identify a strong candidate among choices for a middle school staff. As one principal stated, "When I advertise, I put elementary so I have more flexibility" (18).

> It gives me the flexibility because we have two types of certifications that we use. It gives me the flexibility when I schedule. I like secondary folks for 8th grade math and science positions. They tend to focus on the academics a little more and I need real strong people in those areas. Elementary certified teachers focus more on the child as a whole rather than just the subject matter. A good mix is great. (32)

> Elementary teachers are multicertified so they can teach a variety of courses and can teach one or more subjects. (19)

> We have a lot of elementary trained people and the reason why is that all of us need the flexibility. We can use them in a much more flexible manner than secondary teachers. (27)

Problem Solving

"Young adolescents demonstrate an ability to grapple with complexity, think critically, and deal with information as parts of systems" (Carnegie Council on Adolescent Development, 1989, p. 47). Developmentally responsive middle level leaders realize this and recognize their students' and teachers' desires to participate actively in discovering and creating new solutions to problems. The middle school team approach "emphasizes collaboration, respect for the knowledge base of the professional staff, equalization of power and responsibility in the school, and participation by all" (Capelluti & Stokes, 1991, p. 8). Student empowerment, teacher empowerment, school-based management, and restructuring all contribute to the ideas of ownership and commitment. They promote the concept that decisions should be made at the level closest to the implementation of the decisions. Teachers and students who have more input and whose efforts are acknowledged will be more invested. Three convictions provide the foundations for these organizational arrangements: (1) people need a structure that allows for flexibility, creativity, and accountability; (2) professionals need control over their destiny; and (3) working together rather than in isolation leads to greater productivity (excerpted from Capelluti & Stokes, p. 9). Developmentally responsive middle level leaders are flexible and inclusive in their problem-solving strategies; they "invite everyone into the conversations" and are "willing to live with what the group or committee decides" (12). Their frequent choice of plural pronouns reflects a positive sense of connectedness with others in the school in addition to an openness to more creative problem solving. Responses to questions were peppered with phrases such as "we decided," "our culture is," and "we are prepared to."

> The school culture is changing. They [teachers] used a very authoritarian type of leadership. I am more of a situational leader, more flexible and open. I treat them as professionals. We are moving to a culture of talking and communicating and problem solving together . . . being more flexible. (21)

> I think there's a degree of flexibility that's needed. What you're now looking at is a situation where there are so many variables and so many people. You need to have the ability to balance. (10)

> I think it has much to do with an attitude of how flexible you are . . . how flexible do you do things? Are you willing and able to do things differently than you have for the benefit of kids? (25)

SUMMARY

Developmentally responsive middle level leaders are responsive to the school and the community. They are knowledgeable of and can implement the components of the middle school concept. They act as a responsible catalyst for change, understanding that change requires time, training, trust, and tangible support. And, above all, they are flexible and exhibit a high tolerance for ambiguity and chaos.

The Developmentally Responsive Middle Level Principal

"Almost all educational reform reports have come to the conclusion that the nation cannot attain excellence in education without effective school leadership" (Crawford, 1998, p. 8). We know that effective school leaders: recognize teaching and learning as the main business of school, communicate the school's mission and vision clearly and consistently to all constituents, promote an atmosphere of trust and collaboration, and emphasize professional development (Bauck, 1987; George & Grebing, 1992; Weller, 1999). Despite the consensus that leadership counts, deep philosophical and political disagreements remain about what kind of educational leaders are needed, what knowledge and skills they should possess, and how they should be professional prepared and professionally developed.

As middle level education moves into the 21st century new questions need to be asked and old ones revisited. There is no doubt that middle level principals are essential to current school reform initiatives. Their importance is exacerbated by the current indictments of the middle school movement and the general demand for accountability of schools. Emphasizing this renewed interest in the role of the principal, Olson (2000) wrote:

> After years of work on structural changes, standards and testing and ways of holding students accountable, the education policy world has turned its attention to the people charged with making the system work . . . . But nowhere is the focus on the human element in public education more prevalent than in the renewed recognition of the importance of strong and effective leadership. (p. 1)

In this final chapter we conclude by looking at three areas: (1) the positioning of developmentally responsive leadership in the larger body of literature on school leadership, (2) a model for the developmentally responsive middle level leader, and (3) implications and recommendations for the professional preparation of middle school principals.

MODELS OF SCHOOL LEADERSHIP
AND THE MIDDLE SCHOOL PRINCIPAL

Educational administration researchers have devoted considerable time and energy trying to understand school leadership. Indeed, "leadership is one of the most widely talked about subjects and at the same time one of the most elusive and puzzling" (Cronin, 1993, p. 7). Echoing this belief, Chester Barnard (1948) wrote, "Leadership has been the subject of an extraordinary amount of dogmatically stated nonsense" (p. 80).

Out of this large body of research on leadership comes a variety of distinctly different models or approaches to leadership. Specifically, seven models have dominated contemporary writing about school leadership: (1) instructional leadership, (2) transformational leadership, (3) cultural leadership, (4) moral leadership, (5) participative leadership, (6) managerial leadership, and (7) contingent leadership. Each of these seven models is most distinct with respect to its basic foci and the key assumptions on which it is based. But there are many aspects of these approaches that are quite similar. For example, instructional leadership recognizes the importance of promoting school culture. We now briefly look at each of these seven models in an effort of building a foundation upon which to introduce the model proposed in this book—developmentally responsive leadership. Our intention is not to present an exhaustive discussion of each of these seven models, but to provide a brief introduction along with references for further in-depth study.

Instructional Leadership: The lack of explicit descriptions of instructional leadership (Foster, 1986) makes it difficult to assess the extent to which such leadership means the same things to those writing about it. Examples of models of instructional leadership include Duke (1987), Smith and Andrews (1989), and Hallinger and Murphy (1985). Specifically in Hallinger's work, three broad categories of leadership practice define instructional leadership. These categories include:

defining the school mission, managing the instructional program, and promoting school culture. Associated with these three broad categories are 21 specific practices such as supervision of instruction.

Transformational Leadership: Burns (1978) proposed "transactional" and "transformational" leadership. The main focus of transformational leadership is on the commitments and capacities of organizational members. Higher levels of personal commitment to organizational goals and greater capacities for accomplishing those goals are assumed to result in extra effort and greater productivity. Although the idea of transformational leadership was proposed by Burns (1978), Leithwood (1992; 1999) and his colleagues (Leithwood, Steinbach, & Raun, 1993) have added significantly to our understanding of this leadership model. Leithwood's model (1994) conceptualizes transformational leadership along eight dimensions: (1) building school vision, (2) establishing school goals, (3) providing intellectual stimulation, (4) offering individualized support, (5) modeling best practices and organizational values, (6) demonstrating high performance expectations, (7) creating a productive school culture, and (8) developing structures that foster participation in school decisions.

Cultural Leadership: Numerous scholars have written about "cultural leadership," including Bennis (1989), Schein (1985), Deal and Kennedy (1982), Sarason (1996), and Sashkin and Walberg (1993). Schein (1985) suggested that the most important thing that leaders do is help shape effective culture in which people will complete their work. He contends that culture, "influences the ways in which group members perceive, think, and feel about the world thereby serving to stabilize the world, give meaning to it, and thereby reduce the anxiety that would result if we did not know how to categorize and respond to the environment" (p. 312). In short, an effective and functional school culture steers people in a common direction; provides a set of norms that defines what people accomplish and how; and provides a source of meaning and significance for teachers, students, and administrators.

Moral Leadership: During the 1990s, the normative dimension of leadership has been one of the fastest growing areas of leadership study (Duke, 1996). Those writing about moral leadership argue that values are a central part of all leadership and administrative practice (Bates, 1993; Evers & Lakomski, 1991; Greenfield, 1991; Hodgkinson, 1991).

Hodgkinson (1991) claimed that "values constitute the essential problem of leadership. . . . If there are no value conflicts then there is no need for leadership" (p. 11). In short, the focus of moral leadership is on the values and ethics of the leader, so authority and influence are to be derived from what is perceived to be right and good.

Participative Leadership: Participative leadership (i.e., group, shared, teacher leadership) stresses the decision-making processes of the group. One argument for participative leadership sets forth the belief that participation will enhance organizational effectiveness. Another argument rests its case for participation on democratic principles. In this model, authority and influence are available to any legitimate stakeholder in the school, involving teachers and parents much more in school decision making.

Managerial Leadership: Managerial leadership focuses on the functions, tasks, and behaviors of the leader. It assumes that if these functions are carried out competently, the work of others in the organization will be facilitated and result in an effectively functioning organization. Most approaches to managerial leadership assume that organizational members behave rationally.

Contingent Leadership: Contingent leadership focuses on how leaders respond to the unique organizational circumstances or problems that arise. This model assumes that there are wide variations in the contexts for leadership and that to be effective these contexts require different leadership responses. Also assumed in this model is the belief that those who are in leadership positions have the ability to master a large repertoire of practices.

In addition to these seven models of school leadership we propose an eighth—*developmentally responsive leadership.* Developmentally responsive leadership is grounded in the belief that schools should be organized around the developmental characteristics of the students they educate. A more complete discussion of this model can be found in the next section of this chapter.

In sum, these approaches to conceptualizing school leadership offer eclectic and overlapping perspectives on what should be the focus of the principals' attention and how leadership manifests itself in practice. In looking at the context in which school leadership occurs, we believe that the developmental characteristics of the student have been either ignored or forgotten.

THE DEVELOPMENTALLY RESPONSIVE
MIDDLE LEVEL LEADER: A MODEL
WITH STEVEN J. GROSS, TEMPLE UNIVERSITY

Strange as it may seem, the middle school principal, despite being acknowledged as the key ingredient in achieving an effective middle school, remains the least researched and detailed part of the process of reforming America's middle schools. We now turn the discussion to proposing a model, using the seven themes identified by the middle school principals in this study. It is our hope that this model will prove useful in studying the middle level principalship and assist in more adequately describing and defining developmentally responsive middle level leadership.

We propose a three-dimensional model for the developmentally responsive middle school principal. The features of this model include: (1) responsiveness to the developmental needs of middle grades students, (2) responsiveness to the developmental needs of the faculty who support learning for middle grades students, and (3) responsiveness to the development of the middle school itself as a unique innovating entity. Support for this perspective comes from several supporting theoretical foci. First, recent theoretical writing on "distributed perspective" (Spillane, Halverson, & Diamond, 2001) describes the unit of analysis for the study of schools as "leadership practice in a school unit" (p. 24), rather than the leader acting in isolation. From a distributive perspective, "leadership practice (both thinking and activity) emerges in and through the interaction of leaders, followers and the situation" (p. 27). In our context this means viewing leadership as a principal's interaction with faculty, students, the distinctive nature of the middle school itself, and other key stakeholders. This necessitates connecting with students, their needs, and their current developmental circumstances.

The perspective that a leader's work needs to be seen in a "distributive" way does not necessarily lead to a developmentally responsive approach, although it does clear the path for such a disposition. How will middle level principals frame their school context? Sergiovanni's (1996) use of Tonnies' (1957) "gemeinschaft "(community or moral) and "gesellschaft" (society or formal) as a continuum now becomes relevant.

Although we do not support placing the middle school leader at the extreme of gemeinschaft (i.e., the head of a purely community enterprise), we do believe that leadership at this level of education belongs closer to that end of the continuum and less to the extreme of geselschaft (i.e., the social or formal organization). Our reason is that we are speaking about young people just emerging into adolescence. This is a particularly stressful and momentous developmental period with specific cognitive distinctions (Piaget, 1952) and social and emotional challenges (Erikson, 1964). We believe that working with early adolescents requires a strong orientation toward the ethic of care (Beck, 1994; Noddings, 1992) as its underpinning. This does not exclude challenging academic standards, nor does it preclude middle grades learners from interacting with the demands of the adult world (gesellschaft). We hold that developmentally responsive middle grades leaders are in the best position to help learners at this stage because they will deal with students as they are at a time when recognition of their social, emotional, and intellectual needs is remarkably acute. Developmentally responsive leaders will understand the conditions of their students and use this knowledge with teachers, staff, and families to understand middle grades learners' zone of proximal development (Vygotsky, 1978). Effective scaffolds coming from this analysis are ones that are based upon understanding and responding to middle grades learners' needs.

We believe that this kind of leadership, especially at middle grades, holds the best chance for students to identify with the school (Finn, 1989; Leithwood & Jantzi, 1999) and thus be engaged with the school's learning agenda. In the three-dimensional model we propose, the developmentally responsive middle level principal is responsive to the needs of students, faculty, and the school itself.

**1. Responsiveness to the developmental
needs of middle grades students.**

1.1 Regarding curriculum, instruction, and assessment. There is an urgency to see the clash of middle level social and community needs and academic achievement in a new light—first to acknowledge and understand the nature of the conflict and second to be well-grounded in both relevant curriculum, instruction and assessment, and the related developmental issues of middle grades learners (NMSA, 1995, pp. 35–40). The energy arising from this tension can be used to enhance both quality time to work out the social and emotional needs of this age and to delve more deeply into significant content (i.e., acting out an historic drama).

In this way the learner in the middle grades is not merely "in-between," (a definition of what they are not, neither elementary nor high school—therefore, a weak definition), but a special kind of learner with unique gifts that are short-lived (because no one stays a middle grades student for very long) and therefore, all the more precious. The developmentally responsive principal will think about curriculum, instruction, and assessment and will be able to share that vision with the faculty and stakeholders and develop concrete plans with them. Developmentally appropriate practice requires that both teachers and principals integrate what they know about early adolescent development and the implications of this knowledge for how and when to teach the content of the curriculum and how to assess what students have learned. Specific examples in the literature include a seven-element plan (George et al., 2000 in Clark & Clark, 2000): " 1. Focus on academic achievement in the core curriculum; 2. Daily teacher advisory; 3. Team organization at every grade; 4. Flexible block scheduling; 5. Expanded menu of electives and student activities; 6. Differentiated instruction; and 7. Heterogeneous grouping in science and social studies" (p. 4).

1.2 Regarding school culture and the commitment to community versus bureaucracy. While we find Sergiovanni's (1996) use of community attractive, especially as a metaphor for middle grades leadership, we do not consider middle schools to be simple, easily understood communities. Extending Sergiovanni's metaphor of community, Enomoto (1997) added the notion of nested communities; that is, co-existent spheres within a school or "multiple, overlapping and nested cultures" (p. 529). The developmentally responsive principal must understand and work with these nested communities. Developmentally appropriate practices occur within a context that supports the development of relationships between adults and students, among students, and between teachers and families.

1.3 Regarding responsiveness to the at-risk behaviors unique to middle grades learners. The developmentally responsive middle level principal will understand and help faculty, staff, and families design effective programs relevant to the specific potential at-risk behaviors of students at this age (Carnegie Council on Adolescent Development, 1989; Eccles & Midgley, 1989). Developmental trajectories diverge in early adolescence toward either healthy adjustment or psychopathology (Petersen & Hamburg, 1986). Declines in academic motivation, perceived competence, intrinsic interest in school (Harter, 1981), and self-esteem (Eccles, Midgley, & Adler, 1984) are common, not to mention anxiety, depression, substance abuse, and antisocial behaviors (Hankin, Abramson, Silva, McGee, Moffitt, & Angell, 1998).

1.4 Regarding relationships with families in transition from parenting small children in elementary school to teenagers. The developmentally responsive leader assists parents in understanding their children at this unique stage of their lives. They help in preparing for the physical, emotional, and social changes as well as in understanding the stresses that may lead to at-risk behavior. Moreover, there is a need to engage families and the wider community in understanding the developmental nature of the family itself so that parents can more effectively interact with their middle grades students. These will likely be new behaviors and require parents to be increasingly comfortable with ambiguity (being pushed away by the child and yet still needing to show approval, for instance).

This means that the developmentally responsive middle school principal must understand that there is a developmental cycle of families and where particular families may be, as well as understanding the developmental qualities of parents of middle grades students in their life cycle. Finally, this means understanding how adult learners (i.e., parents, faculty, board members) engage new ideas.

2. Responsiveness to the kind of faculty most likely to connect well and celebrate (not despair of) middle grades learners and understand the developmental needs of this kind of faculty as they mature through their career and life cycle.

We believe that middle schools require a particular kind of teacher; one who is attracted to the energy and complexity of early adolescents and who combines empathy with skills in modeling effective strategies for students of this age. Knowledge of the developmental circumstances of middle grades learners matched with an affinity to curriculum content that is rich, demanding, and highly interactive is also important. A commitment to the middle school's instructional and community-building structures (described earlier)is a high priority as well, especially teaming. The role of developmentally responsive principals is to value these educators and to be highly demanding when the opportunity presents itself to hire new faculty. This also means leadership advocacy for the kind of instruction and organization that will create community. Finally, developmentally responsive leaders need to make a careful study of the career cycle of successful middle grades teachers and apply the lessons of that study to their settings.

3. Responsiveness to the developmental needs of a middle school, operating in a district, guided by a state and likely tested by a national assessment, yet able to see potential for developing and sustaining innovation for middle level education.

Moving outward from the students' developmental needs (described in point one) and the teachers' needs (described in point two), the developmentally responsive middle school leader must see the continued growth of the school itself as an ongoing issue. This means understanding the cycle of school innovation (Gross, 1998) as well as the politics of districts and state governance issues. It also means understanding the unique structures that have been identified for effective middle level education, such as advisory programs, transition programs, interdisciplinary curriculum, exploratory programs, and the like. In this way, leaders are best able to nurture, protect, and defend the hard work that they had helped to initiate and to work toward the school's ultimate goal of improved student achievement.

The literature regarding middle level education and middle school reform is replete with references to "developmental appropriateness" and "developmentally responsive" schools, curriculum, practices, structures, and strategies. Pivotal to this discussion, but conspicuously absent, is the role of middle level leadership in implementing such reform efforts. Although admittedly not exhaustive, we posit that the results from this study begin to define the concept, "developmentally responsive middle level leadership."

An analysis of the qualitative data reveals that leadership responsive to the needs of young adolescents is grounded in the concept of "developmental appropriateness." When examined collectively, the seven emergent themes reveal that developmentally responsive leadership results from the process of making decisions about the well-being and education of children, faculty, and the school itself based on the following kinds of information: "(1) what is known about human development and learning—knowledge of age-related characteristics that permit general predictions within an age range about what activities, materials, interactions, or experiences will be safe, healthy, interesting, achievable, and challenging to young adolescents; (2) what is known about the strengths, interests, and needs of each individual student to be able to adapt for and be responsive to inevitable individual differences; and (3) knowledge of the social and cultural contexts in which children live to ensure that learning experiences are meaningful, relevant, and respectful for the participating children and their families" (National Association for the Education of Young Children, 1997).

Based on the data collected from the middle level principals who participated in this study, we define the *developmentally responsive middle level leader* as one who is:

(1) Responsive to the needs of students:
- understands the intellectual, physical, psychological, social, moral, and ethical characteristics of young adolescents;
- establishes a learning environment that reflects the needs of young adolescents;
- purposely designs programs, policies, curriculum, and procedures that reflect the characteristics of young adolescents;
- understands the relationship between cognitive and affective needs;
- believes that all students can succeed;
- promotes the development of relationships between adults and students, among students, and between teachers and families;
- views parents and the community as partners, not adversaries.

(2) Responsive to the needs of faculty:
- understands the necessity of reconnecting educational administration to the processes of teaching and learning;
- understands the characteristics of successful middle grades teachers;
- is emotionally invested in the job;
- supports teachers in their efforts to understand and respond to the needs of young adolescents;
- shares a vision for continuous organizational improvement and growth;
- governs democratically and collaboratively.

(3) Responsive to needs of the school:
- is knowledgeable of and can implement the components of the middle school concept;
- acts as a responsible catalyst for change and understands that change requires time, training, trust, and tangible support;
- is flexible and able to deal with ambiguity and chaos;

If middle level reform is going to achieve its goals (i.e., a positive educational environment that ensures student cognitive and affective development), middle level principals must come to a more complete understanding of their role in this process. They must acknowledge that different skills and knowledge are necessary for leadership at this level. Being truly "responsive" entails a readiness and willingness to react to suggestions, influences, and appeals; and to reply appropriately and sympathetically. It requires "responding to current challenges, engaging in thoughtful and reflective discussions, and actively and openly embracing the revision and refinement of programs" (Williamson & Johnston, 1999, p. 11). Developmentally responsive middle level leadership recognizes and embraces learners' developmental levels as providing the basis for all school curricular and instructional practices, as well as the overall teaching-learning environment (Manning, 1993).

In a recent article, Neuman and Simmons (2000) discussed reconceptualizing leadership roles for the purpose of improving student achievement. Although they noted the usual strategies, such as developing a shared vision, promoting professional development, and providing a strong accountability system, they do not discuss what we feel to be the most important strategy for principals of middle level schools—being developmentally responsive.

THE PROFESSIONAL PREPARATION OF MIDDLE LEVEL PRINCIPALS

The purpose of most educational administration programs is to prepare school leaders with the knowledge, skills, and commitment to effectively manage and lead a school that is characterized by high teacher satisfaction and efficacy and high student performance. But the efficacy of graduate preparation in educational administration is relatively unstudied. In 1997, Haller, Brent, and McNamara noted that "overall, our reading of the limited literature on this subject suggests that there is little evidence that graduate training increases the effectiveness of school managers" (p. 224).

According to the remarks of the interviewees for this study, formal preparation did not significantly influence their acquisition of essential skills. Even though two-thirds of the principals surveyed received their graduate training in educational administration, many described their programs as inadequate, impractical, and unrealistic. Typical responses include:

Again, I don't think a whole lot of time or effort was spent on the personal side of understanding what's involved in being a principal and dealing with people. It was a lot of theory and not a whole lot of practical application. (03)

I'm not certain about certification. I don't know how much you really learn from courses. You'll forgive me. . . . I have two master's degrees in education—one in curriculum and one in instructional leadership. I'm not really certain how much one learns from being in the classroom and reading all the research. (08)

I think people preparing to be principals need to get out and see what the job is about. Maybe a little more job shadowing is needed. When I was in training there wasn't any of that. Aspiring principals need to get into the schools and see what the job is all about. (15)

Because the practicing middle school principals in this study perceived a deficiency in their overall leadership training, we explored their feelings about the added dimension of working in a middle school. Assuming that the mission of the middle school is to meet the developmental needs (i.e., intellectual, psychological, social, physical, moral, and ethical) of young adolescents, it seems important that educators receive specific preparation in how to interact with students in this distinctive developmental period.

Currently, most university programs in educational leadership prepare prospective school leaders together, making no distinction among levels—elementary, middle, or secondary. The principals whose voices have been heard in this book would like that practice changed. They view middle level education as distinctive. "It's pretty much a whole different animal" (04). Despite their varied backgrounds, many felt similarly and echoed the following comment:

> Well, first of all, they [middle level principals] need to have their own program. Right now you can be a middle level principal with an elementary certificate or a secondary certificate. Specially tailored administrative training at the college or university level should be the number one priority. (01)

The results from a national survey conducted by DeMedio and Mazur-Stewart (1990) regarding educators' attitudes toward middle level certification "support the belief that those preparing to teach middle grade students need special middle grade preparation and appropriate middle grade certification" (p. 70). Even though the middle level principals in this study were not able to reach a consensus regarding the notion of administrative certification, they were able to voice a common concern surrounding their lack of practical preparation focused on middle schools.

As we have noted, the reform literature related to middle level education advocates that effective middle level principals support and promote the establishment of structures that address the developmental needs of young adolescents, such as advisory programs, exploratories, teaming of teachers, transition programs, interdisciplinary teaching and thematic units, and flexible block scheduling. Although almost 80 percent of the principals in this study are currently implementing some of these structures, only 46 percent have had some training. The unfortunate reality, as one principal so bluntly stated, is "you kind of learn by practice at this level" (05). Other principals concurred:

Certainly the training I got did not really address or get into middle school issues at all. (04)

The hardest thing I learned on the job was that I needed to learn more. I knew when I got here and started to work with middle school kids that, if I was going to be a success at all this, I needed to learn what the kids were all about and what techniques worked with them. (07)

But there's no specific training for the middle school principal. And a lot of it is on-the-job experience. So, therefore, if they had middle level certification with the appropriate courses and background, I think principals would be stronger for this particular group of youngsters. (13)

I don't know if being an administrator per se is good enough training to jump into middle school. You must see the middle school model in action in order to understand it. (14)

In short, the results of this study indicate that middle level principals are seeking better preparation that is geared to effectively administering a middle school. They are requesting specific preparation dedicated to the concept of structuring educational programs to meet the unique needs of early adolescents. They are searching for opportunities to learn about themselves and their particular leadership styles. In so doing, they offered three major preservice suggestions for institutions of higher education: (1) prepare middle level principals together in a supportive cohort format; (2) provide real, meaningful middle school internships for prospective administrators and professors alike; and (3) provide the necessary classes that focus on the middle school concept, the nature of the young adolescent, and the implications of this for curriculum, instruction, and assessment. Table C.1 is offered to summarize what the middle level principals who participated in this study would like to see in university-based administrative preparation programs.

Table C.1 The Evolution of Middle Level Principal Preparation Programs

GENERALIZED COMPONENTS OF CURRENT PREPARATION PROGRAMS FROM THE 20th CENTURY	RECOMMENDED PRACTICES TO PREPARE MIDDLE LEVEL LEADERSHIP FOR THE 21st CENTURY
(From)	*(To)*
Generally no distinction among preparation for elementary, middle level, and secondary principalship	Preparation programs with specific courses focused on the middle level and its uniqueness; extended middle level internships and field experiences
Early adolescence as a developmental period viewed as not important to the development of programs, curriculum, or instruction	"Developmental appropriateness" used as a template in the development of all components and functioning of a middle school
Recognizes content as a need and curriculum as "what is"	Understands and applies the components of flexible and block scheduling, integrated curriculum, advisory programs, small learning communities, team teaching, and so forth; Aware of the need to address both cognitive and affective domains of the learner
Uncoupling of administration from teaching and learning	Reconnecting administration to teaching and learning
Preservice principals "trained" to be aware of trends in education and to respond to needs	Establishes the principal as a life-long learner; emphasizes the central role that inservices and professional organizations provide; emphasizes the importance of the principal as "risk-taker"
Trained to manage and efficiently administer a school	Prepares principal to be collaborative in one's approach to leading; to deal with ambiguity and uncertainty
Maintenance of organizational infrastructure	Development of human resources
Excellence is a "state of being"	Excellence is a "state of becoming"

CONCLUDING THOUGHTS

We noted in the introduction to this book that middle schools are under attack. The necessary attention has not been afforded the role of the middle school principal in the reform of middle schools. We know what structures and components need to exist to establish an exemplary middle school, but we have very little idea of how the principal creates, implements, and sustains these structures and components.

Even before the principal's arrival at the school, appropriate attention also has not been given to the preparation of middle school principals. According to Thistle and O'Connor (1992), only five states reported special certification requirements for middle level principals, including Colorado, Kentucky, North Dakota, Rhode Island, and Virginia. Many states have moved toward a generic certification that covers all levels of schooling, K–12. Additionally, after middle school principals complete their formal preparation, there is little attention to their professional development. Indeed, the professional development of school administrators has been described in the literature as "a wasteland," "meager," "neglected," "poverty stricken," "one of the worst slums," and "deplorable." This is especially significant because out of all the educators, principals may have greater needs for renewal than anyone else.

One could legitimately question the reliance of the middle school concept that we accept as gospel, but Felner et al.'s research results (1997) are promising and support the idea that fidelity to the middle school concept will result in improved student performance, both academically and socioemotionally. Additionally, much of what is called for in the middle school concept has been supported by the Effective School's research. But we cannot expect that middle level principals will be capable of implementing middle level reform without the essential and appropriate preservice preparation and continued professional development. Educational administration programs must reverse the trend toward "training" principals as if there is no difference among the administration of elementary, middle, and high schools. Professional organizations and school districts must offer professional development that provides the necessary skills and knowledge related to the implementation and sustainability of the middle level concept. School districts must also provide the necessary resources to support middle school reform.

If, indeed, educational excellence is inextricably coupled with effective school leadership, there is much to be gained from studying the experiences of school leaders. More specifically, given the virtual absence of research specific to middle school leaders, this research provides us with the opportunity to learn from individuals as they live out their professional lives in schools.

Middle school principals who are serious about reforming their schools face a daunting challenge. They need to reconstruct core ideas about their role, and therefore, how they spend their time, set their priorities, seek new knowledge and skills, and situate themselves with respect to teachers and others in the educational community. This process is complicated, takes time, and requires models of good practice. The administrators in this study shared with us their views, hopes, and frustrations; we believe that we have learned much from them. For these insights we are forever grateful.

Identification of Middle Level Principals

Participant Number	Race	Gender	Age	Years of Admin. Exp	Middle School Grades	Middle School Location	Number of Teachers
01	White	Male	50	17	6,7,8	Suburban	80
02	White	Female	54	12	5,6,7,8	Rural	35
03	White	Male	45	13	7,8	Rural	25
04	Black	Male	49	9	6,7,8	Urban	50
05	White	Male	48	1	6,7,8	Urban	45
06	White	Female	48	3	6,7,8	Urban	65
07	White	Male	46	5	7,8	Suburban	60
08	Black	Female	47	1	6,7,8	Suburban	60
09	Black	Female	50	5	6,7,8	Suburban	80
10	White	Male	58	18	7,8	Suburban	60
11	White	Female	35	4	6,7,8	Suburban	50
12	White	Male	41	5	7,8,9	Suburban	75
13	White	Male	62	28	6,7,8	Suburban	60
14	White	Male	56	6	6,7,8,9	Suburban	90
15	White	Male	51	3	7,8,9	Suburban	60
16	White	Male	54	20	6,7,8,9	Suburban	55
17	White	Female	44	3	6,7,8	Urban	55

Participant Number	Race	Gender	Age	Years of Admin. Exp.	Middle School Grades	Middle School Location	Number of Teachers
18	White	Female	56	13	5,6,7,8	Urban	85
19	White	Female	55	21	5,6,7,8	Urban	45
20	White	Male	51	17	6,7,8	Urban	27
21	Black	Female	56	4	6,7,8	Urban	37
22	White	Male	49	19	7,8,9	Suburban	68
23	White	Male	63	33	6,7,8	Suburban	60
24	White	Male	42	16	7,8	Suburban	61
25	White	Male	52	4	7,8,9	Suburban	83
26	White	Male	48	8	6,7,8	Suburban	60
27	White	Female	52	9	6,7,8	Urban	57
28	Black	Male	48	7	6,7,8,9	Suburban	56
29	White	Male	47	16	6,7,8,9	Suburban	51
30	White	Male	57	21	6,7,8,9	Suburban	86
31	Black	Male	59	19	6,7,8	Suburban	42
32	White	Female	52	11	6,7,8	Suburban	44
33	White	Male	48	20	6,7,8	Suburban	51
34	White	Male	50	20	7,8,9	Suburban	135
35	White	Male	54	26	5,6,7,8	Suburban	140
36	White	Male	45	16	6,7,8	Suburban	75
37	Black	Male	27	2	5,6,7,8	Rural	43
38	Black	Female	45	7	6,7	Urban	30
39	White	Male	51	12	6,7,8	Suburban	70
40	White	Male	32	2	K–8	Rural	13
41	White	Male	51	18	6,7,8	Rural	42
42	White	Female	50	24	6,7,8	Rural	25
43	White	Male	44	13	K–8	Rural	25
44	White	Male	32	2	6,7,8	Rural	75

Suggested Middle School References

Readers are encouraged to use this reference list for further research into middle school topics of interest. These selected references are not meant to be exhaustive, but merely a starting point from which to explore more about middle schools. Topics are presented in the following order:

- General Interest
- Young Adolescent Development
- Self-Concept and Self-Esteem in Young Adolescents
- Curriculum
- Interdisciplinary Teaming
- Student and Teacher Relationships
- Teacher Education
- Parent Involvement
- Advisory Programs
- Academic Achievement
- Instruction and Teacher Effectiveness at the Middle Level
- Organization and Organizational Effects in the Middle Level
- Middle School Reform and Implementation
- School Program Evaluation
- Urban and Multicultural Education in the Middle Level

GENERAL INTEREST

Alexander, W. M., & McEwin, C. K. (1989). *Schools in the middle: Status and progress.* Columbus, OH: National Middle School Association.

Anfara, V. A., Jr. (Ed.). (2001). *The handbook of research in middle level education.* Greenwich, CT: Information Age Publishing.

Anfara, V. A., Jr., & Kirby, P. C. (Eds.). (2000). *Voices from the middle: Decrying what is, imploring what could be.* Dubuque, IA: Kendall/Hunt.

Carnegie Council on Adolescent Development. (1989). *Turning points: Preparing American youth for the 21st century.* New York: Carnegie Corporation.

Cohen, J. (Ed.). (1999). *Educating minds and hearts: Social emotional learning and the passage to adolescence.* New York: Teachers College Press.

Dickinson, T. S. (2001). *Reinventing the middle school.* New York: Routledge Falmer.

Eichhorn, D. (1966). *The middle school.* New York: Center for Applied Research.

Epstein, J., & Mac Iver, D. (1990). *Education in the middle grades: National practices and trends.* Columbus, OH: National Middle School Association.

Erb, T. O. (Ed.). (2001). *This we believe and now we must act.* Westerville, OH: National Middle School Association.

George, P. S., & Alexander, W. M. (1993). *The exemplary middle school* (2nd ed.). Fort Worth, TX: Harcourt Brace College Publishers.

George, P. S., & Shewey, K. (1994). *New evidence for the middle school.* Columbus, OH: National Middle School Association.

George, P. S., Stevenson, C., Thomason, J., & Beane, J. (1992). *The middle school—and beyond.* Alexandria, VA: Association for Supervision and Curriculum Development.

Gruhn, W., & Douglass, H. (1956). *The modern junior high school* (2nd ed.). New York: Ronald Press.

Irvin, J. (Ed.). (1997). *What current research says to the middle level practitioner.* Columbus, OH: National Middle School Association.

Jackson, B., & Davis, G. (2000). *Turning points 2000: Educating adolescents in the 21st century.* New York: Teachers College Press/National Middle School Association.

Knowles, T., & Brown, D. (2000). *What every middle school teacher should know.* Portsmouth, NH: Heinemann.

Koos, L. (1927). *The junior high school.* Boston, MA: Ginn and Company.

Lipka, R. P., Lounsbury, J. H., Toepfer, C. F., Vars, G., Alessi, S. P., & Kridel, C. (1998). *The eight year study revisited: Lessons from the past for the present.* Columbus, OH: National Middle School Association.

Lipsitz, J. Y. (1995). *Successful schools for young adolescents.* New Brunswick, NJ: Transaction Publishers.

McEwin, C. K., Dickinson, T. S., & Jenkins, D. M. (1996). *America's middle schools: Practices and progress—A 25 year perspective.* Columbus, OH: National Middle School Association.

National Middle School Association. (1995). *This we believe: Developmentally responsive middle level schools.* Columbus, OH: Author.

National Middle School Association. (1997). *A 21st century agenda.* Columbus, OH: Author.

Noar, G. (1961). *Junior high school: Today and tomorrow.* Englewood Cliffs, NJ: Prentice-Hall.

Rosenzweig, S. (1997). The five-foot bookshelf: Readings on middle-level education and reform. *Phi Delta Kappan, 78*(7), 551–556.

Scales, P. (1996). *Boxed in and bored: How the middle schools continue to fail young adolescents—and what good middle schools do right.* Minneapolis, MN: Search Institute.

Schur, S. (1992). *How to evaluate your middle school.* Columbus, OH: National Middle School Association.

Stevenson, C. (1998). *Teaching ten to fourteen year olds* (2nd ed.). New York: Longman.

VanZandt, L. M., & Totten, S. (1995). The current status of middle level education research: A critical review. *Research in Middle Level Education, 18*(3), 1–26.

Wells, M. C. (1996). *Literacies lost: When students move from a progressive middle school to a traditional high school.* New York: Teachers College Press.

YOUNG ADOLESCENT DEVELOPMENT

Adams, G., Montemayor, R., & Gullotta, T. (Eds.). (1989). *Biology of adolescent behavior and development.* Newbury Park, CA: Sage.

Blos, P. (1979). *The adolescent passage.* New York: International Universities Press.

Caissy, G. A. (1984). *Early adolescence: Understanding the 10 to 15 year old.* New York: Plenum Press.

Eccles, J. S., Midgley, C., Buchanan, C, Wigfield, A., Reuman, D., & Mac Iver, D. (1993). Development during adolescence: The impact of stage/environment fit. *American Psychologist, 48*(2), 90–101.

Erikson, E. (1963). *Childhood and society.* New York: Norton.

Hoose, J. V. (1998). *Young adolescent development and school practices: Promoting harmony.* Columbus, OH: National Middle School Association.

Moore, D. W., Bean, T. W., Birdyshaw, D., & Rycik, J. A. (1999). *Adolescent literacy: A position statement.* Newark, DE: International Reading Association.

Solodow, W. (1999). The meaning of development in middle school. In J. Cohen (Ed.), *Educating minds and hearts: Social emotional learning and the passage into adolescence* (pp. 24–39). New York: Teachers College Press.

SELF-CONCEPT AND SELF-ESTEEM IN YOUNG ADOLESCENTS

Beane, J., & Lipka, R. (1986). *Self-concept and self-esteem and the curriculum.* New York: Teachers College Press.

Beane, J., & Lipka, R. (1987). *When the kids come first: Enhancing self-esteem.* Columbus, OH: National Middle School Association.

Butler, D. A. & Manning, M. L. (1998). *Addressing gender differences in young adolescents.* Olney, MD: Association for Childhood Education International.

Seidman, E., Allen, L., Aber, J. L., Mitchell, C., & Feinman, J. (1994). The impact of school transitions in early adolescence on the self-system and perceived social context of poor urban youth. *Child Development, 65,* 507–522.

CURRICULUM

Alexander, W. A. (1995). *Student oriented curriculum: Asking the right questions.* Columbus, OH: National Middle School Association.

Anfara, V. A., Jr., & Waks, L. (2000). Resolving the tension between academic rigor and developmental appropriateness (Part I). *Middle School Journal, 32*(2), 46–51.

Anfara, V. A., Jr., & Waks, L. (2001). Resolving the tension between academic rigor and developmental appropriateness (Part I). *Middle School Journal, 32*(3), 25–30.

Beane, J. (1991). The middle school: The natural home of integrated curriculum. *Educational Leadership, 49*(2), 943.

Beane, J. (1992). Turning the floor over: Reflections on a middle school curriculum. *Middle School Journal, 23*(3), 34–40.

Beane, J. (1993). *A middle school curriculum: From rhetoric to reality.* Columbus, OH: National Middle School Association.

Berns, B. B., Kantrov, I., Pasquale, M., Makang, D. S., Zubrowski, B., & Goldsmith, L. T. (2000). *Guiding curriculum decisions for middle-grades science*. Newton, MA: Education Development Center.

Brazee, E. N., & Capelluti, J. (1995). *Dissolving boundaries: Toward an integrated curriculum*. Columbus, OH: National Middle School Association.

Capelluti, J., & Brazee, E. (1992). Middle level curriculum: Making sense. *Middle School Journal, 12*(5), 1–5.

Ciardi, M. R., Kantrov, I., & Goldsmith, L. T. (2000). *Guiding curriculum decisions for middle-grades language arts*. Newton, MA: Education Development Center.

Clark, S. N., & Clark, D. C. (1995). *The middle level principal's role in implementing interdisciplinary curriculum*. Reston, VA: National Association of Secondary School Principals.

Dickinson, T. S. (Ed.). (1993). *Readings in middle school curriculum. A continuing conversation*. Columbus, OH: National Middle School Association.

Ellis, A. K., & Stuen, C. J. (1993). *The interdisciplinary curriculum*. Larchmont, NY: Eye On Education.

Hawkins, M. L., & Graham, M. D. (1994). *Curriculum architecture: Creating a place of our own*. Columbus, OH: National Middle School Association.

Kantrov, I., & Goldsmith, L. T. (2000). *Guiding curriculum decisions for middle-grades mathematics*. Newton, MA: Education Development Center.

Lewis, A. C. (n.d.). *Figuring it out: Standards based reform in urban middle schools*. New York: The Edna McConnell Clark Foundation.

Lockledge, A., & Hayn, J. (Eds.). (2000). *Using portfolios across the curriculum*. Columbus, OH: National Middle School Association.

Lounsbury, J. H. (Ed.). (1992). *Connecting the curriculum through interdisciplinary instruction*. Columbus, OH: National Middle School Association.

Nesin, G., & Lounsbury, J. H. (1999). *Curriculum integration: Twenty questions—with answers*. Atlanta, GA: Georgia Middle School Association.

INTERDISCIPLINARY TEAMING

Alspaugh, J. W., & Harting, R. D. (1998). Interdisciplinary team teaching versus departmentalization in middle schools. *Research in Middle Level Education Quarterly, 21*(4), 31–42.

Arhar, J. (1992). Interdisciplinary teaming and the social bonding of middle level students. In J. Irvin (Ed.), *Transforming middle level education: Perspectives and possibilities* (pp. 139–161). Boston: Allyn and Bacon.

Arhar, J., Johnston, J., & Markle, G. (1989). The effects of teaming on students. *Middle School Journal, 20*(3), 21–27.

Arnold, J., & Stevenson, C. (1998). *Teacher's teaming handbook: A middle level planning guide.* Fort Worth, TX: Harcourt Brace College Publishers.

Brown, K. (2000). Interdisciplinary teaming: The cornerstone of community building. *National Forum of Educational Administration and Supervision Journal, 17*(1), 23–45.

Brown, K. (2000). Wise practices in community building: The evolutionary process of team structuring. *Journal of Curriculum and Instruction,* Fall NC-ASCD, 57–74.

Brown, K. (2000). Creating community in middle schools: Interdisciplinary teaming. In V. Anfara & P. Kirby (Eds.), *Voices from the middle: Decrying what is, imploring what could be* (pp. 81–116). Dubuque, IA: Kendall/Hunt.

Brown, K. (2001). Get the big picture of teaming: Eliminate isolation and competition through focus, leadership and professional development. In V. Anfara (Ed.), *The handbook of research in middle level education* (pp. 35–71). Greenwich, CT: Information Age Publishing.

Dickinson, T. S., & Erb, T. O. (Eds.). (1997). *We gain more than we give: Teaming in the middle schools.* Columbus, OH: National Middle School Association.

Erb, T. O., & Doda, N. (1989). *Team organization: Promise, practices and possibilities.* Washington, DC: National Education Association.

Kruse, S., & Louis, K. (1995). Teacher teaming-opportunities and dilemmas. *Brief to principals.* (Brief No. 11). Madison, WI: Center on Organization and Restructuring of Schools.

Merenbloom, E. Y. (1991). *The team process: A handbook for teachers* (3rd edition). Columbus, OH: National Middle School Association.

Mills, R., Powell, R., & Pollack, J. (1992). The influence of interdisciplinary teaming on teacher isolation: A case study. *Research in Middle Level Education, 15*(2), 9–26.

Rottier, J. (1996). *Implementing and improving teaming: A handbook for middle level leaders.* Columbus, OH: National Middle School Association.

STUDENT AND TEACHER RELATIONSHIPS

George, P. S. (1987). *Long-term teacher-student relationships: A middle school case study.* Columbus, OH: National Middle School Association.

TEACHER EDUCATION

Alexander, W. M., & McEwin, C. K. (1988). *Preparing to teach at the middle level.* Columbus, OH: National Middle School Association.

Arth, A. E., Lounsbury, J. H., McEwin, C. K., & Swain, J. H. (1995). *Middle level teachers: Portraits of excellence.* Columbus, OH: National Middle School Association/National Association of Secondary School Principals.

Hart, L., Smith, D., Grynkewich, L., Primm, S., Mizelle, N., Jackson, D., & Mahaffey, M. (1994). *Principles of educating teachers: Middle grades mathematics and science.* Georgia Initiative in Mathematics and Science. Athens, GA: University of Georgia.

Galassi, J. P., Brader-Araje, L., Brooks, L., Dennison, P., Jones, M. G., Mebane, D. J., Parrish, J., Richer, M., White, K., & Vesilind, E. M. (1999). Emerging results from a middle school professional development school: The McDougle-University of North Carolina collaborative inquiry partnership groups. *Peabody Journal of Education, 74*(3–4), 236–253.

Lawton, E. (1993). *The effective middle level teacher.* Reston, VA: National Association of Secondary School Principals.

Manning. M. L. (1989–1990). Contemporary studies of teaching behaviors and their implications for middle level teacher education. *Action in Teacher Education, 11*(4), 1–5.

McEwin, C. K., & Dickinson, T. S. (1995). *The professional preparations of middle level teachers: Profiles of successful programs.* Columbus, OH: National Middle School Association.

McEwin, C. K., Dickinson, T. S., Erb, T. O., & Scales, P. C. (1995). *A vision of excellence: Organizing principles for middle grades teacher preparation.* Columbus, OH: Center for Early Adolescence/National Middle School Association.

National Middle School Association. (1997). *NMSA/NCATE-approved curriculum guidelines handbook.* Columbus, OH: Author.

Scales, P. C. (1992). *Windows of opportunity: Improving middle grades teacher preparation.* Carrboro, NC: Center for Early Adolescence.

Scales, P. C., & McEwin, C. K. (1994). *Growing pains: The making of America's middle school teachers.* Columbus, OH: Center for Early Adolescence/National Middle School Association.

Stahler, T. (1995). A comparative analysis of specifically prepared and generally prepared middle school preservice teachers. *Action in Teacher Education, 17*(3), 23–32.

PARENT INVOLVEMENT

Berla, N. (1992). Parent involvement at the middle school level. *The ERIC Review, 1*(3), 16–20.

Epstein, J. (1987). Parent involvement: What research says to administrators. *Education and Urban Society, 19*(2), 119–136.

Epstein, J. (1987). What principals should know about parent involvement. *Principal, 66*(3), 6–9.

Liederman, J. (1996). Factors associated with parent involvement in the middle grades. Unpublished doctoral dissertation, Lehigh University, Bethlehem, PA.

Loucks, H. E., & Waggoner, J. E. (1998). *Keys to re-engaging families in the education of young adolescents.* Columbus, OH: National Middle School Association.

Myers, J., & Monson, L. (1992). *Involving families.* Columbus, OH: National Middle School Association.

Sui-Chu, E. H., & Willms, J. D. (1996). Effects of parental involvement on eighth-grade achievement. *Sociology of Education, 69,* 126–141.

ADVISORY PROGRAMS

Alexander, W. M., Williams. E., Compton, M., & Prescott, D. (1969). *The emergent middle school* (2nd ed.). New York: Holt, Rinehart, and Winston.

Alexander, W. M., & McEwin, C. K. (1989). Schools in the middle: Progress 1968–1988. *NASSP schools in the middle: A report on trends and practices.* Reston, VA: National Association of Secondary School Principals.

Andrews, B., & Stern, J. (1992). An advisory program—A little can mean a lot! *Middle School Journal, 24*(1), 39–41.

Anfara, V. A., Jr., & Brown, K. M. (2000). An unintended consequence of a middle school reform: Advisories and the feminization of teaching. *Middle School Journal, 31*(3), 26–31.

Association for Supervision and Curriculum Development. (1975). *The middle school we need.* Washington, DC: Author.

Ayres, L. (1994). Middle school advisory programs: Findings from the field. *Middle School Journal, 25*(3), 8–14.

Batsell, G. (1995). Progress toward implementation of developmentally responsive practice in Arizona middle level schools, 1989–1994. Unpublished doctoral dissertation, University of Arizona.

Bunte, A. (1995). Success factors in the implementation of advisory programs in selected Illinois middle schools. Unpublished doctoral dissertation, Southern Illinois University at Carbondale.

Brown, K. M., & Anfara, V. A., Jr. (2001). Competing perspectives on Advisory programs: Mingling or meddling in middle schools. *Research in Middle Level Education Annual, 24,* 1–33.

Brown, K. M., & Anfara, V. A., Jr. (2001). Teacher resistance versus administrative support: Advisory program challenges and opportunities. *National Forum of Applied Educational Research Journal, 15*(1), 13–36.

Cole, C. (1992). Nurturing a teacher advisory program. Columbus, OH: National Middle School Association.

Cole, C. (1994). Teachers' attitudes before beginning a teacher advisory program. *Middle School Journal, 25*(5), 3–7.

Connors, N. (1986). A case study to determine the essential components and effects of an advisor/advisee program in an exemplary middle school. Unpublished doctoral dissertation. Florida State University, Tallahassee, FL.

Connors, N. (1991). Teacher advisory: The fourth "r". In J.L. Irvin (Ed.), *Transforming middle level education: Perspectives and possibilities* (pp.162–178). Needham Heights, MA: Allyn and Bacon.

Dale, P. (1993). Leadership, development, and organization of an advisor/advisee program: A comparative case study of two middle schools. Unpublished doctoral dissertation, Fordham University, New York.

Galassi, J., Gulledge, S. A., & Cox, N. D. (1997). Middle school advisories: Retrospect and prospect. *Review of Educational Research, 67*(3), 301–338.

Galassi, J. P., Gulledge, S. A., & Cox, N. D. (1998). *Advisory: Definitions, decisions, directions.* Columbus, OH: National Middle School Association.

Gill, J., & Read, E. (1990). The experts comment on advisor-advisee programs. *Middle School Journal, 21*(5), 31–33.

Hall, G. (1905). *Adolescence: Its psychology and its relations to physiology, anthropology, sociology, sex, crime, religion, and education* (Vol. II). New York: Appleton & Co.

Hertzog, C. (1992). Middle level advisory programs: From the ground up. *Schools in the Middle, 2*(1), 23–27.

Hoverston, C., Doda, N., & Lounsbury, J. H. (1991). *Treasure chest: A teacher advisory source book.* Columbus, OH: National Middle School Association.

James, M. (1986). *Adviser-advisee programs: Why, what, and how.* Columbus, OH: National Middle School Association.

Jenkins, J. (1977). The teacher-adviser: An old solution looking for a problem. *NASSP Bulletin, 61,* 29–34.

Jenkins, J. M., & Daniel, B. S. (2000). *Banishing anonymity: Middle and high school advisement programs.* Larchmont, NY: Eye On Education.

Krathwohl, D. (1964). *Taxonomy of educational objectives, Handbook II: Affective domain.* New York: McKay.

Lee, S. (1995). Implementing the teacher advisory program at the middle school: A case study of technical, normative and political perspectives of change. Unpublished doctoral dissertation, University of California, Los Angeles.

Mac Iver, D. (1990). Meeting the needs of young adolescents: Advisory groups, interdisciplinary teaching teams, and school transition programs. *Phi Delta Kappan, 71*(6), 458–464.

McEwin, C. K. (1981). Establishing teacher-advisory programs in middle level schools. *Journal of Early Adolescence, 1,* 337–348.

Mosidi, M. (1994). A qualitative study of the process of implementing the advisor-advisee program in a school setting. Unpublished doctoral dissertation. The University of Toledo.

Phillips, R. (1986). *Making advisory programs work.* Tampa, FL: Wiles, Bondi Associates.

Putbrese, L. (1989). Advisory programs at the middle level—The students' response. *NASSP Bulletin, 73*(514), 111–115.

Sardo-Brown, D., & Shetlar, J. (1994). Listening to students and teachers to revise a rural advisory program. *Middle School Journal, 26*(1), 23–25.

Stamm, M., & Nissman, B. (1979). *Improving middle school guidance.* Boston, MA: Allyn and Bacon.

Trubowitz, S. (1994, Winter). The quest for the good advisor-advisee program. *Middle Ground,* 3–5.

Van Hoose, J. (1991). The ultimate goal: A/A across the day. *Midpoints, 2*(1), 1–7.

Watson, D. (1980). *Caring for strangers.* London: Routledge & Kegan Paul.

ACADEMIC ACHIEVEMENT

Arnold, J. (1997). High expectations for all: Perspective and practice. *Middle School Journal, 28*(3), 51–53.

Aseltine, J. M. (1993). Performance assessment: Looking at the "real" achievement of middle level students. *Schools in the Middle, 3*(1), 27–30.

Backes, J., Ralston, A., & Ingwalson, G. (1999). Middle level reform: The impact on student achievement. *Research in Middle Level Education Quarterly, 22*(3), 43–57.

Bowers, R. S. (2000). A pedagogy of success: Meeting the challenges of urban middle schools. *The Clearing House, 73*(4), 235–238.

Bradley, A., & Manzo, K. K. (2000, October 4). The weak link. *Education Week, 20*(5), 3–8.

Felner, R., Jackson, A. W., Kasak, D., Mulhall, P., Brand, S., & Flowers, N. (1997). The project on high performance learning communities: Applying the land-grant model to school reform. *Phi Delta Kappan, 78*(7), 520–527.

Felner, R., Jackson, A. W., Kasak, D., Mulhall, P., Brand, S., & Flowers, N. (1997). The impact of school reform for the middle grades: A longitudinal study of a network engaged in Turning Points-based comprehensive school transformation. In R. Takanishi & D. A. Hamburg (Eds.), *Preparing adolescents for the twenty-first century: Challenges facing Europe and the United States* (pp. 38–69). Cambridge, UK: Cambridge University Press.

Hatch, H., & Hytten, K. (1997). Working together to improve middle school student achievement. *Journal of Staff Development, 18*(2), 6–12.

Hough, D., & Sills-Briegel, T. (1997). Student achievement and middle level programs, policies, and practices in rural; America: The case of community-based versus consolidated organizations. *Journal of Research in Rural Education, 13*(1), 64–70.

Lee, V. E., & Smith, J. B. (1993). Effects of school restructuring on the achievement and engagement of middle-grade students. *Sociology of Education, 66*(3), 164–187.

Russell, J. F. (1997). Relationship between the implementation of middle-level program concepts and student achievement. *Journal of Curriculum and Supervision, 12*(2), 152–168.

Stevenson, C., & Erb, T. O. (1998). How implementing Turning Points improves student outcomes. *Middle School Journal, 30*(1), 49–52.

Vassallo, P. (1990). Muddle in the middle: Are middle schools the right choice for the wrong reason? *The American School Board Journal, 177*(9), 26–27, 37.

Williamson, R. D., Johnston, J. H., & Kanthak, L. M. (1995). The agenda: The achievement agenda for middle level schools. *Schools in the Middle, 5*(2), 6–9.

Williamson, R. D. (1996). Modifying structure: A resource for improved student achievement at the middle level. *NASSP Bulletin, 80*(578), 17–23.

INSTRUCTION AND TEACHER
EFFECTIVENESS AT THE MIDDLE LEVEL

Atwell, N. (1998). *In the middle: New understandings about writing, reading, and learning* (2nd ed.). Portsmouth, NH: Boynton/Cook Publishers.

Bradford, D. J. (1999). Exemplary urban middle school teachers' use of the five standards of effective teaching. *Teaching and Change, 7*(1), 53–78.

Hibbard, K. M. (2000). *Performance-based learning and assessment in middle school science.* Larchmont, NY: Eye On Education.

Leutzinger, I. (Ed.). (1998). *Mathematics in the middle.* Columbus, OH: National Council of Teachers of Mathematics/National Middle School Association.

Lustig, K. (1996). *Portfolio assessment: A handbook for middle level teachers.* Columbus, OH: National Middle School Association.

Morretta, T. M., & Ambrosini, M. (2000). *Practical approaches for teaching reading and writing in middle schools.* Newark, DE: International Reading Association.

Schurr, S., & Forte, I. (1993). *The definitive middle school guide.* Nashville, TN: Incentive Publications.

ORGANIZATION AND ORGANIZATIONAL
EFFECTS IN THE MIDDLE LEVEL

Brown, K., & Roney, K. (2003). "Turning points" to success: A case study of reform implementation in a charter middle school. *Middle School Journal, 34*(3).

Brown, K., & Anfara, V. (Spring 2002). The walls of division crumble as ears, mouths, minds, and hearts open: A unified profession of middle level administrators and teachers. *International Journal of Leadership in Education, 5*(1), 33–49.

Clark, S. N., & Clark, D. C. (1994). *Restructuring the middle level school: Implications for school leaders.* Albany, NY: SUNY Press.

Eccles, J. S., Lord, S., & Midgley, C. (1991). What are we doing to early adolescents? The impact of educational contexts on early adolescents. *American Journal of Education, 99,* 521–539.

Offenberg, R. M. (2001). The efficacy of Philadelphia's K-to-8 schools compared to middle grades schools. *Middle School Journal, 32*(4), 23–29.

Rettig, M. D., & Canady, R. L. (2000). *Scheduling strategies for middle schools.* Larchmont, NY: Eye On Education.

Warren, L. L., & Payne, B. D. (1997). Impact of middle grades' organization on teacher efficacy and environmental perceptions. *The Journal of Educational Research, 90*(5), 301–308.

Williamson, R. D. (1998). *Scheduling middle level schools: Tools for improved student achievement.* Reston, VA: National Association of Secondary School Principals.

MIDDLE SCHOOL REFORM AND IMPLEMENTATION

Cuban, L. (1992). What happens to reforms that last? The case of the junior high school. *American Educational Research Journal, 29*(2), 227–251.

Hatch, H., & Hytten, K. (1997). *Mobilizing resources for district-wide middle-grades reform.* Columbus, OH: National Middle School Association.

Lipsitz, J., Mizell, M. H., Jackson, A. W., & Austin, L. M. (1997). Speaking with one voice: A manifesto for middle-grades reform. *Phi Delta Kappan, 78*(7), 533–540.

Mac Iver, D., & Epstein, J. L. (1993). Middle grades research: Not yet mature, but no longer a child. *The Elementary School Journal, 93*(5), 519–533.

Manning, M. L., Lucking, R., & MacDonald, R. H. (1995). What works in urban middle schools. *Childhood Education, 71*(4), 221–224.

Mergendoller, J. R. (1993). Introduction: The role of research in the reform of middle grades education. *The Elementary School Journal, 93*(5), 443–446.

Osuch, J. (1997). Beyond early childhood: Restructuring efforts at the middle level. *Childhood Education, 73*(5), 282–285.

White, G. P. (1993). Revolution in the middle: Recasting the middle level learning system. *Middle School Journal, 25*(1), 8–12.

SCHOOL PROGRAM EVALUATION

Fitzpatrick, K. A. (1998). *Indicators of school quality.* Schaumburg, IL: National Study of School Evaluation.

Schurr, S. L. (2000). *How to evaluate your middle school: A practitioner's guide for an informal program evaluation.* Columbus, OH: National Middle School Association.

Watson, C. R. (1999). *Best practices from America's middle schools.* Larchmont, NY: Eye On Education.

URBAN AND MULTICULTURAL EDUCATION IN THE MIDDLE LEVEL

Wilson, B. L., & Corbett, H. D. (2001). *Listening to urban kids: School reform and the teachers they want.* Albany, NY: SUNY Press.

Alexander, W. M. (1965). The junior high: A changing view. In G. Hass & K. Wiles (Eds), *Readings in curriculum* (pp.418–425). Boston: Allyn and Bacon.

Alexander, W. M. (1969). *The emergent middle school.* New York: Holt, Reinhart, and Winston.

Alexander, W. M., & George, P. (1981). *The exemplary middle school.* New York: Holt, Reinhart, and Winston.

Alexander, W. M., & McEwin, C. K. (1989). *Schools in the middle: Status and progress.* Columbus, OH: National Middle School Association.

Anderman, E., & Urdan, T. (1995). A multilevel approach to middle-level reform. *Principal, 74,* 26–28.

Argyris, C., & Schon, D. (1978). *Organizational learning: A theory of action perspective.* Reading, MA: Addison-Wesley.

Arhar, J. (1992). Interdisciplinary teaming and the social bonding of middle level students. In J. L. Irvin (Ed.), *Transforming middle level education: Perspectives and possibilities* (pp.139–161). Boston: Allyn & Bacon.

Arnold, J., & Stevenson, C. (1998). *Teachers' teaming handbook: A middle level planning guide.* Fort Worth, TX: Harcourt Brace College Publishers.

Arth, A. (1985). *An agenda for excellence.* Reston, VA: National Association of Secondary School Principals.

Arth, A., Lounsbury, J., McEwin, C., Swaim, J., & Eighty-three Successful Middle Level Educators. (1995). *Middle level teachers: Portraits of excellence.* Columbus, OH: National Middle School Association and National Association of Secondary School Principals.

Ashton, P., & Webb, R. (1986). *Making a difference: Teachers' sense of efficacy and student achievement.* New York: Longman.

Association for Supervision and Curriculum Development. (1975). *The middle school we need.* Washington, DC: Author.

Balfanz, R., & Mac Iver, D. (1998). The school district's role in creating high performing urban middle schools. Unpublished paper commissioned by Carnegie Corporation of New York for the Turning Points 2000 book project. Johns Hopkins University.

Barnard, C. I. (1948). *Organizations and management.* Cambridge, MA: Harvard University Press.

Barth, R. S. (1986). Principal centered professional development. *Theory Into Practice, 25*(3), 156–160.

Barth, R. S. (1988). School: A community of leaders. In A. Lieberman (Ed.), *Building a professional culture in schools* (pp.129–147). New York: Teachers College Press.

Bates, R. (1993). On knowing: Cultural and critical approaches to educationaladministration. *Educational Management and Administration, 21*(3), 171–176.

Bauck, J. (1987). Characteristics of the effective middle school principal. *NASSP Bulletin, 71*(500), 90–92.

Bauer, S. (1992). Myth, concensus, and change. *Executive Educator, 14*(7), 26–28.

Beane, J. (1990). Affective dimensions of effective middle school. *Educational Horizon,* 109–112.

Beane, J., & Lipka, D. (1987). *When kids come first: Enhancing self-esteem.* Columbus, OH: National Middle School Association.

Beck, L. (1994). *Reclaiming educational administration as a caring profession.* New York: Teachers College Press.

Beck, L., & Murphy, J. (1993). *Understanding the principalship.* New York: Teachers College Press.

Bennis, W. (1989). *On becoming a leader.* Reading, MA: Addison-Wesley.

Blase, J., & Blase, J. (1994). *Empowering teachers: What successful principals do.* Thousand Oaks, CA: Corwin Press, Inc.

Bolman, L., & Deal, T. (1993). *The path to school leadership: A portable mentor.* Newbury Park, CA: Corwin Press, Inc.

Bossing, N. (1954). A junior high designed for tomorrow. *The Clearing House, 9.*

Bowers, R. (1995). Early adolescent social and emotional development: A constructivist perspective. In. M.Wavering (Ed.), *Educating young adolescents: Life in the middle* (pp.79–109). New York: Garland.

Bowman, B. (1994). Home and school: The unresolved relationship. In S. L. Kagan & B. Weissbourd (Eds.), *Putting families first: America's family support movement and the challenge of change* (pp.51–72). San Francisco, CA: Jossey-Bass.

Bradley, J. (1998, April 15). Muddle in the middle. *Education Week, 17*(31), 38–42.

Bradley, A., & Manzo, K. (2000, October 4). The weak link. *Education Week* (supplement), 3–8.

Brough, J. (1995). Middle level education: An historical perspective. In M. Wavering (Ed.), *Educating young adolescents: Life in the middle* (pp.27–51). New York: Garland.

Brough, J. (1997). Home-school partnerships: A critical link. In J. Irvin (Ed.), *What current research says to the middle level practitioner* (pp.265–274). Columbus, OH: National Middle School Association.

Brown, K. (1999). Creating community in middle schools: Interdisciplinary teaming and advisory programs. Unpublished dissertation, Temple University, Philadelphia, PA.

Bulach, C. (1993). A measure of openness and trust. *People in Education, 1*(4), 382–392.

Bulach, C., Boothe, D., & Pickett, W. (1997). *Mistakes educational leaders make,* 1–10, (ED 404 737).

Burke, M. A. (2001). Recruiting and using volunteers in meaningful ways in secondary schools. *National Association of Secondary School Principals Bulletin, 85*(627), 46–52.

Burke, M. A., & Picus, L. O. (2001). *Developing community-empowered schools.* Thousand Oaks, CA: Corwin Press.

Burkhardt, R. (1997). Teaming: Sharing the experience. In T. Dickinson & T. Erb (Eds.), *We gain more than we give: Teaming in middle schools* (pp.163–184). Columbus, OH: National Middle School Association.

Burns, J. (1978). *Leadership.* New York: Harper & Row.

Butterfield, D., & Muse, I. (1993). District administrators' assumptions about principal training: Fact or fiction? *Connections, 2*(1), 4–5.

California State Department of Education. (1987). *Caught in the middle: Educational reform for young adolescents in California public schools.* Sacramento, CA: Author.

Capelluti, J., & Stokes, D. (Eds.). (1991). *Middle level education: Programs, policies, & practices.* Reston, VA: National Association of Secondary School Principals.

Carnegie Council on Adolescent Development. (1989). *Turning points: Preparing youth for the 21st century.* New York: Carnegie Corporation.

Carnegie Task Force on Teaching as a Profession. (1986). *A nation prepared: Teachers for the 21st century.* New York: Carnegie Forum on Education and the Economy.

Carpenter, W., & Anglin, J. (2000). Behold a curricular symphony, a sonata, or an etude performed by undisciplined musicians? *Middle School Journal, 31*(3), 38–43.

Causey, T., & Wood, S. (2000). Parents in the middle. In V. Anfara & P. Kirby (Eds.), *Voices from the middle: Decrying what is, imploring what could be.* Dubuque, IA: Kendall/Hunt.

Clark, S. (1995). What leadership skills do principals really need? *School Administrator, 52,* 8–11.

Clark, S., & Clark, D. (1987). Interdisciplinary teaming programs: Organization, rationale, and implementation. *Schools in the middle: A report on trends and practices.* Reston, VA: National Association of Secondary School Principals.

Clark, S., & Clark, D. (1989, February). School restructuring: A leadership challenge for middle-level administrators. *Schools in the middle: A report of trends and practices.* Reston, VA: National Association of Secondary School Principals.

Clark, S., & Clark, D. (1994). *Restructuring the middle level school: Implications for school leaders.* Albany, NY: State University of New York.

Clark, S., & Clark, D. (2000). Developmentally responsive curriculum and school-based reform: Implications for middle level principals. *NASSP Bulletin, 84,* 1–13.

Comer, J. (1988). School-parent relationships that work: An interview with James Comer. *Harvard Education Letter, 4*(6), 4–6.

Commission on the Reorganization of Secondary Education. (1918). *Cardinal principles of secondary education.* Washington, DC: Department of the Interior, Bureau of Education.

Compton, M., & Hawn, H. (1993). *Exploration: The total curriculum.* Columbus, OH: National Middle School Association.

Conrad, W. (1992). Profile of the effective teacher for the 21st century. *Illinois Association for Supervision and Curriculum Development, 29*(2), 17–18.

Cotton, K., & Savard, W. G. (1980). The principal as instructional leader. Paper presented for the Alaska Department of Education Office of Planning and Research by the Audit and Evaluation Program. Portland, OR: Northwest Educational Laboratory.

Cotton, K., & Wikelund, K. (1989). Parent involvement in education. *School Improvement Research Series* [Online]. Available: http://www.nwrel.org/scpd/sirs/3/cu6.html.

Crawford, J. (1998). Changes in administrative licensure: 1991–1996. *UCEA Review, 39*(3), 8–10.

Cronin, T. E. (1993). Reflections on leadership. In W. E. Rosenbach & R. L. Taylor (Eds.), *Contemporary issues in leadership* (pp.7–25). Boulder, CO: Westview Press.

Cuban, L. (1983). Effective schools: A friendly but cautionary note. *Phi Delta Kappan, 64*(10), 695–696.

Darling-Hammond, L. (1997). *The right to learn: A blueprint for creating schools that work.* San Francisco, CA: Jossey-Bass.

Darling-Hammond, L., & McLaughlin, M. (1995). Policies that support professional development in an era of reform. *Phi Delta Kappan, 76*(8), 597–604.

Davidson, N. (1989). Small group cooperative learning in mathematics: A review of research. In N. Davidson & R. Dees (Eds.), *Research in small group cooperative learning in mathematics.* Reston, VA: National Council of Teachers of Mathematics.

Davies, M. (1995). The ideal middle level teacher. In M. Wavering (Ed.), *Educating young adolescents: Life in the middle* (pp.149–169). New York: Garland.

Deal, T. (1985). Cultural change: Opportunity, silent killer, or metamorphosis. In R. Killmann, M. Saxton, & R. Serpa (Eds.), *Gaining control of the corporate culture* (pp.292–331). San Francisco, CA: Jossey-Bass.

Deal, T. E., & Kennedy, A. (1982). *Corporate cultures.* Reading, MA: Addison-Wesley.

DeBruyn, R. L. (1996). Why administrative assistance and positive reinforcement are necessary on a weekly basis for teachers? *The MASTER Teacher.* Manhattan, KS: The Master Teacher, Inc.

Delgado, M. (1999). Lifesaving 101: How a veteran teacher can help a beginner. *Educational Leadership, 56*(8), 27–29.

DeMedio, D., & Mazur-Stewart, M. (1990). Attitudes toward middle grade certification: A national survey. *NASSP Bulletin, 74,* 64–70.

Department of Education Statistics. (1995). *Digest of education statistics.* Washington, DC: National Center for Education Statistics.

Desimone, L. (1999). Linking parent involvement with student achievement: Do race and income matter? *The Journal of Educational Research, 93*(1), 11–30.

DiBiase, W. J., & Queen, J. A. (1999). Middle school social studies on the block. *Clearing House, 72*(6), 377–384.

Doda, H., George, P., & McEwin, K. (1987). The current truths about effective schools. *Middle School Journal, 18*(3), 3–5.

Dorman, G. (1981). *Middle grades assessment program.* Chapel Hill, NC: Center for Early Adolescence, University of North Carolina.

Driscoll, M. (1995). Thinking like a fish: The implications of the image of school community for connections between parents and schools. In P. W. Cookson & B. Schneider (Eds.), *Transforming schools* (pp.209–236). New York: Garland.

Duke, D. L. (1987). *School leadership and instructional improvement.* New York: Random House.

Duke, D. L. (1996). Perception, prescription and the future of school leadership. In K. Leithwood et al. (Ed.), *The international handbook of educational leadership and administration* (pp.841–872). The Netherlands: Kluwer Academic Publishers.

Duke, D. L., & Canady, R. (1991). *School policy.* New York: McGraw-Hill.

Eccles, J., & Midgley, C. (1989). Stage-environment fit: Developmentally appropriate classrooms for young adolescents. In R. E. Ames & C. Ames (Eds.), *Research on motivation in education* (Vol.3, pp.139–181). New York: Academic Press.

Eccles, J., Midgley, C., & Adler, T. (1984). Grade-related changes in school environment: Effects on achievement motivation. In J. H. Nicholls (Ed.), *The development of achievement motivation* (Vol.3, pp.283–331). Greenwich, CT: JAI.

Eccles, J., & Wigfield, A. (1997). Young adolescent development. In J. L. Irvin (Ed.), *What current research says to the middle level practitioner* (pp.15–29). Columbus, OH: National Middle School Association.

Eichhorn, D. (1966). *The middle school.* New York: The Center for Applied Research in Education.

Enomoto, E. (1997). Schools as nested communities: Sergiovanni's metaphor extended. *Urban Education, 32,* 512–531.

Epstein, J. (1995). School, family, and school partnerships: Caring for the children we share. *Phi Delta Kappan, 79,* 701–712.

Epstein, J. L., & Mac Iver, D. J. (1989). *Education in the middle grades: Overview of a national survey of practices and trends.* Baltimore, MD: Johns Hopkins University Center for Research on Elementary and Middle Schools.

Epstein, J. L., & Mac Iver, D. J. (1990). *Education in the middle grades: Overview of national practices and trends.* Columbus, OH: National Middle School Association.

Epstein, J. L., & Salinas, K. (1992). New directions in the middle grades. *Childhood Education, 67*(5), 285–292.

Erb, T., & Stevenson, C. (1999). From faith to facts: Turning Points in action – Fostering growth inducing environments for student success. *Middle School Journal, 30*(4), 63–67.

Ericksen, S. (1984). *The essence of good teaching: Helping students learn and remember what they learn.* San Francisco: Jossey-Bass.

Erikson, E. (1964). *Childhood and society.* New York: Norton.

Evans, P., & Mohr, N. (1999). Professional development for principals: Seven core beliefs. *Phi Delta Kappan, 80*(7), 530–532.

Evers, C. W., & Lakomski, G. (1991). *Knowing educational administration: Contemporary methodological controversies in educational administration.* New York: Pergamon Press.

Felner, R., Jackson, A. W., Kasak, D., Mulhall, P., Brand, S., & Flowers, N. (1997). The impact of school reform for the middle grades: A longitudinal study of a network engaged in Turning Points-based comprehensive school transformation. In R. Takanishi & D. A. Hamburg (Eds.), *Preparing adolescents for the twenty-first century: Challenges facing Europe and the United States* (pp.38–69). Cambridge, UK: Cambridge University Press.

Finn, J. D. (1989). Withdrawing from school. *Review of Research, 59,* 117–143.

Foster, W. (1986). *The reconstruction of leadership.* Victoria, Australia: Deakin University Press.

Fugate, J. (1970). An analysis of the implementation year of a junior high school modular schedule as it relates to teachers, students, parents, achievement and grades. Unpublished dissertation, University of Idaho.

Fullan, M. (1991). *The new meaning of educational change.* New York: Teachers College Press.

Fullan, M. (1995). The limits and potential of preofessional development. In T.R. Guskey & M.Huberman (Eds.), *Professional development in education* (pp.253–267). New York: Teachers College Press.

Fullan, M. (1998). Leadership for the 21st century – breaking the bonds of dependency. *Educational Leadership, 55*(7), 6–10.

Fullan, M. (1999). Leading change in professional learning communities. *Education Update, 41*(8), 1–4.

Fullan, M., & Hargreaves, A. (1991). *What's worth fighting for?: Working together for your school.* Toronto: Ontario Public School Teachers' Federation.

Fullan, M., & Hargreaves, A. (1996). *What's worth fighting for in your school?* New York: Teachers College Press.

Fullan , M., & Miles, M. (1992). Getting reform right: What works and what doesn't. *Phi Delta Kappan, 73*(1), 744–752.

George, P. S. (1990). From junior high to middle school—principals' perspectives. *NASSP Bulletin, 74,* 86–94.

George, P. S., & Alexander, W. M. (1993). *The exemplary middle school* (2nd ed.). New York: Holt, Reinhart and Winston.

George, P. S., & Grebing, W. (1992). Seven essential skills of middle level leadership. *Schools in the Middle, 1*(4), 3–11.

George, P. S., & Oldaker, L. L. (1985). *Evidence for the middle school.* Columbus, OH: National Middle School Association.

George, P. S., & Stevenson, C. (1989). The "very best teams" in the "very best" middle schools as described by middle school principals. *TEAM, 3,* 6–17.

Giammetteo, M. C., & Giammetteo, D. W. (1981). *Forces on leadership.* Reston, VA: National Association of Secondary School Principals.

Glickman, C. (1998). *Revolutionizing America's schools.* San Francisco, CA: Jossey-Bass.

Goodman, P. S., & Associates. (1986). *Designing effective work groups.* San Francisco: Jossey-Bass.

Graves, L. (1992). Cooperative learning communities: Context for a new vision of education and society. *Journal of Education, 2,* 57–79.

Greenfield, T. (1991). Re-forming and re-valuing educational administration: Whence and when cometh the phoenix? *Educational Management and Administration, 19*(4), 200–217.

Grooms, M. (1967). *Perspectives on the middle school.* Columbus, OH: Merrill.

Gross, S. J. (1998). *Staying centered: Curriculum leadership in a turbulent era.* Alexandria, VA: Association for Supervision and Curriculum Development.

Gruhn, W., & Douglass, H. (1956). *The modern junior high* (2nd edition). New York: Ronald Press.

Hall, G. S. (1905). *Adolescence: Its psychology and its relations to physiology, anthropology, sociology, sex, crime, religion and education* (Vol.II). New York: Appleton & Co.

Haller, E., Brent, B., & McNamara, J. (1997). Does graduate training in educational administration improve America's schools? *Phi Delta Kappan, 79*(3), 222–227.

Hallinger, P., & Murphy, J. (1985). Assessing the instructional management behavior of principals. *Elementary School Journal, 86*(2), 217–247.

Hankin, B., Abramson, L., Silva, P., McGee, R., Moffitt, T., & Angell, K. (1998). Development of depression from preadolescence to young adulthood: Emerging gender differences in a 10-year longitudinal study. *Journal of Abnormal Psychology, 107,* 128–140.

Harter, S. (1981). A new self-report scale of intrinsic versus extrinsic orientation in the classroom: Motivational and informational components. *Developmental Psychology, 17,* 300–312.

Hatch, H., & Hytten, K. (1997). Working together to improve middle school student achievement. *Journal of Staff Development, 18*(2), 6–12.

Hipp, K. A. (1996). Teacher efficacy: Influence of principal leadership behavior. Paper presented at the annual conference of the American Educational Research Association, New York.

Hipp, K. (1997). The impact of principals in sustaining middle school change. *Middle School Journal, 28*(2), 42–45.

Hodgkinson, C. (1991). *Educational leadership: The moral art.* Albany, NY: SUNY Press.

Hoover-Dempsey, K., & Sandler, H. (1997). Why do parents become involved in their children's education? *Review of Educational Research, 67*(1), 3–42.

Hough, D., & Irvin, J. (1997). Setting a research agenda. In J. Irvin (Ed.), *What current research says to the middle level practitioner* (pp.351–356). Columbus, OH: National Middle School Association.

Hoy, W., & Sabo, D. (1998). *Quality middle schools: Open and healthy.* Thousand Oaks, CA: Corwin Press.

Hunter, M., & Morrison, S. (1978). What's going on around here? Twelve principals talk about preservice, inservice, and other woes. *National Elementary School Principal, 57*(3), 9–19.

Iannaccone, L., & Jamgochian, R. (1985). High performing curriculum and instructional leadership in the climate of excellence. *NASSP Bulletin, 69*, 28–35.

Jackson, A. W., & Davis, G. A. (2000). *Turning points 2000: Educating adolescents in the 21st century.* New York: Teachers College Press/National Middle School Association.

Johnson, N. (1994). Educational reforms and professional development of principals: Implications for universities. *The Journal of Educational Administration, 32*(2), 5–20.

Johnson, J., Dupuis, V., Musial, D., & Hall, G. (1994). *Introduction to the foundations of American education.* Needham Heights, MA: Allyn and Bacon.

Johnston, J., & Markle, G. (1986). *What research says to the middle level practitioner.* Columbus, OH: National Middle School Association.

Johnston, J. H., & Williamson, R. (1998). Listening to four communities: Parents and public concerns about middle level schools. *NASSP Bulletin, 82*(597), 44–52.

Jones, J. (1997). Mature teams at work: Benchmarks and obstacles. In T. Dickinson & T. Erb (Eds.), *We gain more than we give: Teaming in middle schools* (pp.205–228). Columbus, OH: National Middle School Association.

Keefe, J., Clark, D., Nickerson, N., & Valentine, J. (1983). *The middle level principalship: Volume II: The effective middle level principal.* Reston, VA: National Association of Secondary School Principals.

Keefe, J. W., Valentine, J. W., Clark, D. C., & Irvin, J. L. (1994). *Leadership in middle level education: Leadership in successfully restructuring middle level schools.* Reston, VA: National Association of Secondary School Principals.

Kellough, R. D., & Kellough, N. G. (1999). *Middle school teaching: A guide to methods and resources* (3rd ed.). Upper Saddle River, NJ: Merrill.

Kilcrease, A. (1995). Principals' perceptions of the functions and characteristics of middle schools in Mississippi. Paper presented at the Annual Meeting of the Mid-South Educational Research Association. November 8–10, Biloxi, MS.

Kilgore, J., Webb, R., & the Faculty and Staff of Coral Springs Middle School, Broward County, Florida. (1997). Making shared decision making work. *Middle School Journal, 28*(5), 3–13.

Killion, J., & Hirsh, S. (1998, March 18). A crack in the middle. *Education Week,* pp.44–48.

Kohut, S. (1990). A quality middle school: What makes the difference? *Educational Horizon, 48*(3), 107–108.

Koos, L. (1927). *The junior high.* Boston, MA: Ginn and Company.

Kramer, L. (1992). Young adolescents' perceptions of school. In J.L. Irvin (Ed.), *Transforming middle level education: Perspectives and possibilities* (pp.28–45). Boston: Allyn & Bacon.

Lange, J. (1993). Site-based shared decision making: A resource for restructuring. *NASSP Bulletin, 76*(549), 98–107.

Lawton, E. (1993). *The effective middle level teacher.* Reston, VA: National Association of Secondary School Principals.

Leithwood, K. (1992). The move toward transformational leadership. *Educational Leadership, 49*(5), 8–12.

Leithwood, K. (1994). Leadership for school restructuring. *Educational Administration Quarterly, 30*(4), 498–518.

Leithwood, K. (1999). *Changing leadership for changing times.* Bristol, PA: Taylor Frances.

Leithwood, K., & Jantzi, D. (1999). The relative effects of principal and teacher sources of leadership on student engagement with school. *Educational Administration Quarterly, 35*(5), 679–706.

Leithwood, K., Steinbach, R., & Raun, T. (1993). Superintendents' group problem-solving processes. *Educational Administration Quarterly, 29*(3), 364–391.

Lightfoot, S. (1983). *The good high school: Portraits of character and culture.* New York: Basic Books.

Lincoln, Y., & Guba, E. (1985). *Naturalistic inquiry.* Beverly Hills, CA: Sage.

Lipsitz, J. (1984). *Successful schools for young adolescents.* New Brunswick, NJ: Transaction Books.

Little, J. W. (1993). Teachers' professional development in a climate of educational reform. *Educational Evaluation and Policy Analysis, 15*(2), 129–151.

Lockhart, J. (1997). Confessions of a high school teacher. *The English Journal, 86,* 105–108.

Lounsbury, J. (1960). How the junior high school came to be. *Educational Leadership, 18,* 145–147.

Lounsbury, J., & Clark, D. (1990). *Inside grade eight: From apathy to excitement.* Reston, VA: National Association of Secondary School Principals.

Lounsbury, J., & Vars, G. (1978). *A curriculum for the middle school years.* New York: Harper & Row.

Lucas, C. (1999). Developing competent practitioners. *Educational Leadership, 56*(8), 45–48.

Lumsden, L. (1994). *Student motivation to learn.* Office of Educational Research and Improvement, U.S. Department of Education.

Mac Iver, D. (1990). Meeting the needs of young adolescents: Advisory groups, interdisciplinary teaching teams, and school transition programs. *Phi Delta Kappan, 71*(6), 458–464.

Maeroff, G. (1990). Getting to know a good middle school: Shoreham Wading River. *Phi Delta Kappan, 71*(7), 505–511.

Manning, M. L. (1993). *Developmentally appropriate middle level schools.* Wheaton, MD: Association for Childhood Education International.

Marjoribanks, J. (1996). Ethnicity, family achievement syndrome, and adolescents' aspirations: Rosen's framework revisited. *Journal of Genetic Psychology, 157,* 349–359.

McKay, J. (1995). *Schools in the middle: Developing a middle-level orientation.* Thousand Oaks, CA: Corwin Press.

McNeal, R. (1999). Parental involvement as social capital: Differential effectiveness on science achievement, truancy, and dropping out. *Social Forces, 78*(1), 117–144.

Meier, D. (1995). *The power of their ideas: Lessons for America from a small school in Harlem.* Boston: Beacon Press.

Mergendoller, J. (1993). Introduction: The role of research in the reform of middle grades education. *The Elementary School Journal, 93,* 443–446.

Merriam, S. B. (1988). *Case study research in education: A qualitative approach.* San Francisco, CA: Jossey-Bass.

Merz, C., & Furman, G. (1997). *Community and schools: Promise and paradox.* New York: Teachers College Press.

MetLife (1998). Building family-school partnerships: Views of teachers and students. *The Metropolitan Life Survey of The American Teacher 1998.* New York: Louis Harris and Associates, Inc.

Mezirow, J., & Associates. (1990). *Fostering critical reflection in adulthood: A guide to transformative and emancipatory learning.* San Francisco: Jossey Bass.

Mid-Atlantic Eisenhower Consortium for Mathematics and Science Education. (1997). *A sourcebook of 8th-grade findings: TIMSS.* Philadelphia, PA: Research for Better Schools.

Miles, M. (1986). *Research findings on the stages of school improvement.* New York: Center for Policy Research.

Milgram, J. (1992). A portrait of diversity: The middle school student. In J. L. Irvin (Ed.), *Transforming middle level education: Perspectives and possibilities* (pp.16–26). Needham Heights, MA: Allyn and Bacon.

Mills, R. (1997). Expert teaching and successful learning at the middle level: One teacher's story. *Middle School Journal, 29*(1), 30–39.

Montgomery, J. (1995). From K-3 to junior high: A principal's challenge. *Principal, 74,* 94–99.

Mulhall, P., Mertens, S., & Flowers, N. (2001). How familiar are parents with middle level practices? *Middle School Journal, 33*(2), 57–61.

Murphy, J. (1991). *Restructuring schools: Capturing and assessing the phenomena.* New York: Teachers College Press.

Murphy, J. (1999). Reconnecting teaching and school administration: A call for a unified profession. *The UCEA Review, XL*(2), 1–7.

National Association for the Education of Young Children. (1997). Statement of the position. http://www.naeyc.org/resources/position_statement/ dap2.htm

National Association of Elementary School Principals. (1990). *Principals for 21st century schools.* Alexandria, VA: Author.

National Association of Secondary School Principals Council on Middle Level Education. (1985). *An agenda for excellence at the middle level.* Reston, VA: Author.

National Education Association. (1899). *Journal of proceedings and addresses.* Denver, CO: Author.

National Education Association. (1965). *Middle schools.* Washington, DC: Author.

National Education Goals Panel. (1998). *National education goals report: Building a nation of learning 1998.* Washington, DC: Author.

National Forum to Accelerate Middle-Grades Reform. (2000). [Vision statement]. Retrieved July 31, 2001, from http://www.mgforum.org.

National Middle School Association. (1982). *This we believe.* Columbus, OH: Author.

National Middle School Association. (1992). *This we believe.* Columbus, OH: Author.

National Middle School Association. (1995). *This we believe: Developmentally responsive middle schools.* Columbus, OH: Author.

National Middle School Association. (1997). *A 21st century research agenda: Issues, topics & questions guiding inquiry into middle level theory & practice.* Columbus, OH: Author.

National Middle School Association. (2000). National Middle Schools Association's position statement on academic achievement. On-line: http://www.nmsa.org/resources/pospapacachieve.html

National Network of Partnership Schools [Online]. Available: http://scov.csos.jhu.edu/p2000/p2000.html.

Neufeld, B. (1997). Responding to the expressed needs of urban middle school principals. *Urban Education, 31*(5), 490–510.

Neuman, M., & Simmons, W. (2000). Leadership for student learning. *Phi Delta Kappan, 82*(1), 9–12.

Newmann, F. (1991). *What is a structured school? A framework to clarify ends and means.* Madison, WI: University of Wisconsin.

Noddings, N. (1992). *The challenge to care in schools: An alternative approach to education.* New York: Teachers College Press.

Office of Educational Research and Improvement. (1998). *Family involvement in children's education: Successful local approaches.* Washington, DC: US Department of Education.

Olson, L. (1990, April 4). Parents as partners: redefining the social contract between families and schools. *Education Week, 9,* 17–24.

Olson, L. (2000). Policy focus converges on leadership: Several major new efforts under way. *Education Week, 19*(17), 1, 16–17.

Palmer, P. (1993). *To know as we are known: Education as a spiritual journey.* New York: HarperCollins.

Palmer, P. (1997). The heart of a teacher: Identity and integrity in teaching. *Change, 29*(6), 15–21.

Payne, M. J., Conroy, S., & Racine, L. (1998). Creating positive school climates. *Middle School Journal, 30*(2), 65–67.

Payzant, T. W., & Gardner, M. (1994). Changing roles and responsibilities in a restructuring school district. *NASSP Bulletin, 78*(560), 8–17.

Petersen, A., & Hamburg, B. (1986). Adolescence: A developmental approach to problems and psychopathology. *Behavior Therapy, 17,* 480–499.

Piaget, J. (1952). *The origins of intelligence in children.* New York: International Universities Press.

Pollio, H. (1991, Fall). Hermes in the classroom: Interpreting what expert teachers say about teaching (*Teaching-Learning Issues,* No. 69). Learning Research Center, University of Tennessee.

Renchler, R. (1992). *School leadership and student motivation.* (ED 346 558).

Robbins, P., & Alvy, H. (1995). *The principal's companion: Strategies and hints to make the job easier.* Thousand Oaks, CA: Corwin Press.

Rogers, S., & Renard, L. (1999). Relationship-driven teaching. *Educational Leadership, 57*(1), 34–37.

Roney, K. (2000). Characteristics of effective middle level teachers: A case study of principal, teacher, and student perspectives. Unpublished doctoral dissertation, Temple University, Philadelphia, PA.

Rost, J. C. (1991). *Leadership for the twenty-first century.* New York: Praeger.

Rubinstein, R. (1990). A teacher's view of the quality principal. *Educational Horizons, 66,* 151–152.

Sanders, M. (1996). Building family partnerships that last. *Educational Leadership, 54*(3), 61–66.

Sanders, M. (2001). Schools, families, and communities partnering for middle level students' success. *NASSP Bulletin, 85*(627), 53–61.

Sanders, M., & Simon, B. (1999). Progress and challenges: Comparing elementary, middle and high school in the National Network of Partnership Schools. Paper presented at the American Education Research Association Annual Conference in Montreal.

Saphier, J., & King, M. (1985). Good seeds grow in strong cultures. *Educational Leadership, 42*(6), 67–74.

Sarason, S. B. (1990). *The predictable failure of educational reform.* San Francisco: Jossey Bass.

Sarason, S. B. (1996). *Barometers of change: Individual educational social transformation.* San Francisco: Jossey-Bass.

Sashkin, M., & Walberg, H. (1993). *Educational leadership and school culture.* Berkley, CA: McCutchan.

Scales, P. (1992). *Windows of opportunity: Improving middle grades teacher preparation.* Carrboro, NC: Center for Early Adolescence.

Schein, E. (1985). *Organizational culture and leadership.* San Francisco: Jossey-Bass.

Schmidt, D. (1988). Do squirrely kids need squirrely administrators? *Principal, 68,* 48–53.

Seller, W. (1993). New images for the principal's role in professional development. *Journal of Staff Development, 14*(1), 22–26.

Sergiovanni, T. (1996). *Leadership for the schoolhouse: How is it different? Why is it important?* San Francisco: Jossey-Bass.

Shedd, J., & Bacharach, S. (1991). *Tangled hierarchies: Teachers as professionals and the management of schools.* San Francisco, CA: Jossey-Bass.

Short, P., & Greer, J. (1997). *Leadership in empowered schools: Themes from innovative efforts.* Upper Saddle River, NJ: Merrill/Prentice Hall.

Silver, E. (1998). *Improving mathematics in middle school: Lessons from TIMSS and related research.* Washington, DC: Department of Education, Office of Educational Research and Improvement.

Slavin, R., & Madden, N. (1989). What works for students at risk: A research synthesis. *Educational Leadership, 46,* 4–13.

Smith, S., & Scott, J. (1990). *The collaborative school: A work environment for effective instruction.* Eugene, OR: ERIC Clearinghouse on Educational Management/National Association of Secondary School Principals.

Smith, W. F., & Andrews, R. L. (1989). *Instructional leadership: How principals make a difference.* Alexandria, VA: Association for Supervision and Curriculum Development.

Speck, M. (1999). *The principalship: Building a learning community.* Upper Saddle River, NJ: Merrill/Prentice Hall.

Spillane, J., Halverson, R., & Diamond, J. (2001). Investigating school leadership practice: A distributed perspective. *Educational Researcher, 30*(3), 23 28.

Spindler, J., & George, P. (1984). Participatory leadership in the middle school. *The Clearing House, 7,* 293–295.

Stevenson, C., & Erb, T. (1998). How implementing Turning Points improves student outcomes. *Middle School Journal, 30*(1), 49–52.

Tarter, J. (1995). Middle school climate, faculty trust, and effectiveness: A path analysis. *Journal of Research and Development in Education, 29,* 41–49.

Thistle, M., & O'Connor, J. (1992). Teachers' and principals' attitudes. Paper presented at the annual meeting of the California Educational Research Association. San Francisco, CA.

Tomlinson, C. (1999). *The differentiated classroom: Responding to the needs of all learners.* Alexandria, VA: Association for Supervision and Curriculum Development.

Tomlinson, C., Moon, T., & Callahan, C. (1998). How well are we addressing academic diversity in the middle school? *Middle School Journal, 29*(3), 3–11.

Tonnies, F. (1957). *Gemeinschaft unt Gesellschaft.* (Community and Society). (C.P. Loomis, Ed. and Trans.). New York: HarperCollins.

Trimble, S., & Miller, J. (1996). Creating, invigorating, and sustaining effective teams. *NASSP Bulletin, 80*(584), 35–40.

Valentine, J., Clark, D., Irvin, J., Keefe, J., & Melton, G. (1981). *Leadership in middle level education.* Reston, VA: National Association of Secondary School Principals.

Valentine, J., Clark, D., Nickerson, N., Jr., Keefe, J. (1981). *The middle level principalship; A survey of middle level principals and programs* (Vol. I). Reston, VA: National Association of Secondary School Principals.

Valentine, J., Maher, M. C., Quinne, D., & Irvin, J. (1999). The changing roles of effective middle level principals. *Middle School Journal, 30*(5), 54–56.

Vygotsky, L. (1978). *Mind and society: The development of higher psychological processes.* Cambridge, MA: Harvard University Press.

Wasser, J., & Bresler, L. (1996). Working in the interpretive zone: Conceptualizing collaboration in qualitative research teams. *Educational Researcher, 25*(5), 5–15.

Weller, L. D. (1999). *Quality middle school leadership: Eleven central skill areas.* Lancaster, PA: Technomic Publishing.

Wheatley, M. J. (1992). *Leadership and the new science: Learning about organization from an orderly universe.* San Francisco: Berrett-Koehler Publishers.

Whitaker, T. C., & Valentine, J. W. (1993). How do you rate? *Schools in the Middle, 3*(2), 21–24.

Whitmire, R. (1998, March). Middle schools targeted as the weak link in education chain. *The Reporter,* pp.A1, A4.

Wiles, J., & Bondi, J. (1981). *The essential middle school.* Columbus, OH: Merrill.

Williamson, R. (1991). Leadership at the middle level. In J. Capelluti & D. Stokes (Eds.). *Middle level education: Programs, policies, and practices* (pp.36–41). Alexandria, VA: National Association of Secondary School Principals.

Williamson, R., & Johnston, J. H. (1999). Challenging orthodoxy: An emerging agenda for middle level reform. *Middle School Journal, 30*(4), 10–17.

Willis, S. (1999). The accountability question. *Education Update, 41*(7), 1, 4–5, 8.

Wolfe, P. (1998). Revisiting effective teaching. *Educational Leadership, 56*(3), 61–64.

Zembe, R. (1985, August). The Honeywell studies: How managers learn to manage. *Training, 22.*

Index

About the Authors

Kathleen M. Brown is assistant professor of educational leadership at the University of North Carolina at Chapel Hill. Prior to receiving her Ed.D. from Temple University in educational administration and policy studies, Brown taught middle school and served as an elementary and middle school principal in Philadelphia, Pennsylvania and Camden, New Jersey. She brings to the university 15 years of teaching, administrative, and research experience. She is involved at the national level with the National Middle School Association (NMSA), the American Educational Research Association (AERA), and the University Council for Educational Administration (UCEA). Her research interests involve effective, site-based servant leadership that marries theory, practice, and social justice issues in tearing down walls and building a unified profession of educators. She approaches education from an ethic of care and works toward changing the metaphor of schools from hierarchical bureaucracies to nurturing communities. Brown is interested in middle school reform and often researches best practices in providing developmentally responsive educational programs.

Vincent A. Anfara Jr. is associate professor of educational leadership at the University of Tennessee, Knoxville. He received his Ph.D. in educational administration from the University of New Orleans in 1995. Before entering the professorate, he taught for 25 years in both middle and high schools in Louisiana and New Mexico. He has published widely on middle school advisory programs, middle school reform, and the middle level principalship. He coedited the book entitled *Voices from the Middle: Decrying What Is; Imploring What Could Be* with Peggy Kirby (2000). He serves as the series editor of *The Handbook of*

Research in Middle Level Education. Currently he is the president of AERA's special interest group, known as Research in Middle Level Education, and a member of NMSA's research committee.